"HEAR ME OUT"

GEORGE C. WALLACE

DROKE HOUSE, *Publishers*

ANDERSON, S. C.

———

Distributed by

GROSSET AND DUNLAP

51 Madison Avenue, New York, N. Y.

G. & D. No. 6716

Library of Congress Catalog Card Number: 68-13825

Published by DROKE HOUSE, Publishers
Anderson, S. C.

MANUFACTURED IN THE UNITED STATES OF AMERICA

ACKNOWLEDGMENTS

All quotations in this volume are reprinted with the contractual permission of George C. Wallace, their author.

The publishers gratefully acknowledge permission from the publications listed below, to reprint statements by Governor Wallace from copyrighted articles and interviews.

Copyright Acknowledgements:

CHRISTIAN CENTURY. Copyrighted 1965, Christian Century Foundation; reprinted by permission from April 21, 1965 issue of The Christian Century.

LIFE MAGAZINE. Column "The View from Here" by Loudon Wainwright. Copyrighted. Reprinted by permission.

NATIONAL REVIEW. Interview with James Jackson Kilpatrick. Copyright, National Review. Reprinted by permission.

NEW YORK TIMES. Copyright 1967/1966 by The New York Times Company. Reprinted by permission.

NEWSWEEK. Copyright, Newsweek. Reprinted by permission.

NORTH AMERICAN NEWSPAPER ALLIANCE. Interview with Vera Glaser. Copyright August 28, 1967. Reprinted by permisssion.

REPORTER. Copyright 1966 by The Reporter Magazine Company. Reprinted by permission.

TIME MAGAZINE. Reprinted by permission.

U. S. NEWS & WORLD REPORT. From Copyrighted articles and interviews, April 20 and June 1, 1964; March 20, 1967, in U. S. News and World Report.

$\cdot\cdot$ A $\cdot\cdot$

ALABAMA

... **Education.** Alabamians want educational opportunities for their children equal to the best in the nation. Such a goal is consistent with Southern traditions, aspirations and Southern pride. I pledge my administration will take whatever measures are necessary to make our school system second to none in the South. We will have full school terms. We will have more school buildings. We will pay our teachers better. I will go before the legislature, I will speak before the citizens of our state. I will do whatever is necessary to bring us out of this educational crisis.

Speech
Altoona, Alabama
1962 *Campaign for*
Governor of Alabama

... **Negro Employment.** We have seen created since I have been governor about 75,000 jobs in Alabama and about 26,000 of

these jobs have been for members of the
Negro race.

*Reply to Petition
to the Governor
Selma-to-Montgomery
Civil Rights March
March* 19, 1965

. . . Negro Opportunities. We are having
the largest educational program in Alabama's
history. I am building eight junior colleges and
trade schools today for the exclusive use of
the Negro race. I am working for a free text
book program through the twelfth grade. We
are the only state in the South that doesn't
have that, because I want black and white
children both to have books to go to school,
because many of them do not . . . we have had
more new industry to come to our state, more
new jobs for Negroes. We don't have an unemployment problem among Negroes in our
state. I am working for educational enhance-
ment. That is the solution to these problems.
We are going to stop dropouts in Alabama
among members of the Negro race.

*Interview
Face The Nation
(CBS-TV)
March* 14, 1965

AMERICA

...The true brotherhood of America, of respecting the separateness of others and uniting in effort, has been so twisted and distorted from its original concept that there is small wonder that communism is winning the world.

Inaugural Address
Montgomery, Ala.
January 14, 1963

...Americans should stand up for America. ⌐

Interview
March 20, 1967

...It's about time we quit worrying about what they (foreign countries) think of us and let them start worrying about what we think of them. It's our money they are spending. We don't have to apologize for America. We have more civil rights per square inch here than they have in a square mile behind the Iron Curtain.

Speech
Butler University
Indianapolis, Indiana
1964 Primary Campaign

...**Diversity.** The United States is made up of separate races, separate religions, separate

7

denominations, separate cultures, separate languages and separate states. We have always been a unity of the many divergencies, for this has been our secret of dynamics, our will to creativeness. From these fountainheads of differences have come the diversities of free men before the open forum of honest controversy and rich contribution from which decisions are arrived at that speak the will and the wisdom of free and diverse people. But now there are those who would amalgamate us into a unit of one, subservient to a powerful central government, with laws designed to equalize us into the common denominator necessary for a slave people. If we follow this course of making government our master, we shall soon discover, and too late, that everything that is not forbidden by law, is required by law — by law that can change in a moment at the whim of a few powerful men in central government.

Speech
Whitewater State College
Wisconsin
March 23, 1964

. . . This nation was never meant to be a unit of one, but a unity of the many. This is the exact reason our freedom-loving forefathers established many states, insuring that no central power could gain master government control.

Inaugural Address
Montgomery, Alabama
January 14, 1963

... Foreign Policy. I am getting tired of our country always worrying about what somebody thinks of us. We just ought to do the right thing in the matter of foreign policy and if it's not liked, well we just can't help it.

Speech
Rose Polytechnic
Institute
Terre Haute, Indiana
Spring, 1967

... Politics. Basically speaking, the people all over the country are the same. They are still for the American system and they are tired of folks sponsoring movements to change the concept of American Government for political reasons only.

Interview
U. S. News and
World Report
June 1, 1964

ARBITRATION

...I'm not what you'd call a great U.N. supporter, but I'm not against the basic idea. The idea of settling disputes around a conference table is good. I've settled some that way myself—just get both sides together, and say, you settle this thing.

Interview with
James Jackson Kilpatrick
National Review
April 18, 1967

· · B · ·

BACKLASH

. . . I don't believe there is a backlash in this country against people because of color. I think that is a journalistic expression. I think it was coined by the news media. I think there is a backlash against the theoreticians and the bureaucrats in national government who are trying to solve problems that ought to be solved on the local level . . . There is not any backlash among the mass of American people against anybody because of color. There is a backlash against big government in this country.

Interview
Meet The Press
(NBC-TV)
April 23, 1967

BIBLE

. . . The Supreme Court has made it against the law to read the Bible in public schools. Certain northern newspapers and magazines, in an effort to be derogatory against Alabama

11

said "Alabama is in the Bible Belt . . . "
What's so wrong about being for the Bible?

Speech
Run-off Election
Campaign
1962

BIBLE READING

. . . We are going to keep on reading the
Bible in Alabama (public schools)—I don't
care what the Supreme Court says.

Speech
Indiana University
April 23, 1964

BIG GOVERNMENT

. . . Democratic government has changed its
direction. It now appears in the dress of a
welfare state where government referees all
rights and the individual is subject to the
caprice and whim of an autocratic, all-powerful government structure.

Speech
University of Cincinnati
February 11, 1964

. . . I am not a racist as many people have
been led by the left-wing, liberal press, to
believe. We in Alabama, along with ever-

12

growing and imposing groups of other Americans, have made it known that we are concerned over the continuing trend toward autocratic government—that we will not willingly relinquish the basic tenets of our system. We ask no more or no less than that you attempt to understand that our actions are based on a premise of acting lawfully under the Constitution of the United States. My campaign is based on an attack on the fact that the federal government in Washington is reaching into every facet of society and encroaching on the rightful powers of the state. Through the so-called Civil Rights Bill, Washington is planning an additional invasion of the lawful prerogatives of the state. It is reaching into homes, schools, businesses, farms and labor.

News Conference
Terre Haute, Indiana
1964 *Presidential*
Primary Campaign

. . . I think there is an ever-growing tendency on the part of the American people to be fed up with big government.

Interview
Meet The Press
(*NBC-TV*)
April 23, 1967

13

. . . Big government has destroyed freedom and liberty in America.

Interview
Newsweek
May 8, 1967

. . . If one of the national parties were to take stock of the trend and attitude of the people, and say, "Yes, we see. We are going to turn back local control to the States. We are going to get out of everybody's lives"— then that would suit me. But that doesn't appear to be in the offing.

Interview
U. S. News and
World Report
March 20, 1967

BIRACIAL COMMITTEES

. . . There are biracial committees in every large city in the United States, biracial committees in New York, Philadelphia and Chicago. They are in many cities in this state (Alabama), and yet we have demonstrations today continuously in other cities of the United States. So a biracial committee, in my judg-

ment, doesn't necessarily mean there will be a
cessation of demonstrations.

Interview
Face The Nation
(CBS-TV)
March 14, 1965

BUREAUCRATS

. . . Our lives are being taken over by bureaucrats and most of them have beards.

Interview
Newsweek
May 8, 1967

15

$\cdot\cdot \mathbf{C} \cdot\cdot$

CENTRALIZED POWER

... All through history you find that in any country where you centralize power in the hands of the central government, people lose their freedoms.

> *Interview*
> *U. S. News and*
> *World Report*
> *March* 20, 1967

... People are concerned about the effort of the Government in Washington to grasp for more and more power over the lives of the people.

> *Interview*
> *U. S. News and*
> *World Report*
> *April* 20, 1964

CITIES

... **North and South.** You can walk safely on the streets in Birmingham and in Montgomery (Alabama), our State's capital. You can walk anyplace at any time—either race can—without fear of molestation. But that's not true in the citadels of "liberalism" in the nation's capital or New York City or places of that sort.

Interview
U. S. News and
    World Report
March 20, 1967

CIVIL RIGHTS

... We don't oppose the civil rights of anybody. Any citizen of this country is entitled to civil rights regardless of their race or color. And they are guaranteed in the Constitution of our country.

Speech
Rose Polytechnic Institute
Terre Haute, Indiana
Spring, 1967

CIVIL RIGHTS ACT

... I am not against non-discrimination, but I am against the government of the United States in the name of civil rights trying to control the property rights of people, trying to c o n t r o l the seniority list of labor

17

unions, trying to control the apprenticeship list of labor unions, and I feel that the so-called Civil Rights Act is not in the interests of any citizen of this country, regardless of their race. I think it is an infringement upon the property right system, but I want to see that all people in this country, regardless of their color, do well.

> *Interview*
> *Meet The Press*
> *(NBC-TV)*
> *April* 23, 1967

...I would advocate modifications in the Civil Rights Bill.

> *Interview*
> *Meet The Press*
> *(NBC-TV)*
> *April* 23, 1967

... **Public Accommodations.** Under the public accommodation section (of the Civil Rights Bill) they say you have a right to exclude anyone from your boarding house if it's five rooms or under, but if it's six or more rooms, it's unlawful. It's immoral to reject somebody or select your clientele with six or more rooms but it's not immoral with five rooms or under. If it's a moral issue involved

it ought to be one room or all rooms under
the public accommodation section.

Speech
Earlham College
Richmond, Indiana
April 20, 1964

CIVIL RIGHTS BILL

... Many people have come to see that the
civil rights bill before Congress would tend
to destroy the system that has made us what
we are, and is not in the interest of anybody—regardless of race, color, creed or national origin.

Interview
U. S. News and
    World Report
April 20, 1964

... There are not two sides to the civil right
controversy, unless you're for unbridled federal executive power. If the (Civil Rights)
bill becomes law, there will be no need for
state governments, for all power will be shift-
ed to Washington.

News Conference
Columbus, Ohio
February 12, 1964

19

... (The Civil Rights Bill) is a back-door open-occupancy bill. Now if you want an open-occupancy bill in your state, have it. Let them pass it in the state legislature, or your city government body. Why has Washington put an open-occupancy bill on you? Why can't you decide that question for yourselves? I feel that a man who owns a home which is his castle ought to be able to sell it to people with blue hair and green eyes only. It's his house. And whenever a bill is passed which says your grandmother can be put in jail without a trial by jury because she refused to rent a room to somebody and the court believed that she did it because of race, color, creed or national origin, then you've destroyed a most basic civil right in this country.

Speech
Earlham College
Richmond, Indiana
April 20, 1964

... This Civil Rights Bill doesn't create a single new job in the United States except 10,000 jobs for bureaucrats in Washington, D. C.   (32

Speech
Earlham College
Richmond, Indiana
April 20, 1964

...Most people think that the so-called Civil Rights Bill is aimed at the people of Mississippi and Alabama, but this bill is aimed at every homeowner, every business and every labor union and every farm and every school in the State of Indiana and all other states.

Speech
Earlham College
Richmond, Indiana
April 20, 1964

...If (the Civil Rights Bill) does pass, you're going to have a police state. You will have a police state. You're going to have a federal police force to enforce the provisions of this act. And when it passes and becomes a law, there's going to be a great hue and cry raised . . . in every state in the Union for its repeal two or four years from now.

Speech
Earlham College
Richmond, Indiana
April 20, 1964

...A secret vote would defeat the Civil Rights Bill.

News Conference
Columbus, Ohio
February 12, 1964

. . . If the Civil Rights Bill had been put to a referendum, it would have been defeated.

Interview
U. S. News and
World Report
June 1, 1964

. . . The way I see it, we'll have either an absolute police state to enforce the provisions of the (Civil Rights) bill, or a state of total law violation. This would be something like the prohibition amendment until the government became tired of allowing a pressure group to push everyone around. You will see that such sentiment as this will increase as the bill is enforced.

News Conference
Cincinnati, Ohio
February 11, 1964

. . . Every Congressman who voted for this (Civil Rights) bill voted to turn every state over to the Federal government. They voted to give the government power over the running of every business and every labor union in the country.

News Conference
Cincinnati, Ohio
February 11, 1964

22

... There is virtually no aspect of business life which will not be affected by the public accommodations section of this (Civil Rights) bill. If you are engaged in any profession where you offer your professional services, you cannot refuse to serve anyone without fear of violating this act. If an establishment offers goods and services for sale, hire or use and is open to the public, then it is subject to federal regulation. It is difficult to find a single area of the bill which does not pose a tyrannical threat to our whole concept of government and society.

Speech
University of Cincinnati
February 11, 1964

... The Civil Rights Bill is a prime example of what propaganda, misrepresentation, and misunderstanding can do to a governmental structure. Passage of this bill through a cloud of emotionalism will extend federal control over business, industry and individuals.

Speech
U. C. L. A.
January 9, 1964

... The right to sell your property to anyone you want to will be taken away if the Civil Rights Bill passes the Congress . . . The right to reject applicants for employment because of lack of qualifications is another right that will be taken away from store owners.

Speech
University of Oregon
January 13, 1964

... (The Civil Rights Bill) is a political, not a moral issue. It is, in reality, a grab for federal power.

Speech
Indiana University
April 23, 1964

...**Ambiguousness.** Under this (Civil Rights) bill they can come in and enjoin a man, a business man or labor union, even before the act's violated. They can, if they "feel" that you are about to violate the act. Now how in the name of common sense are we going to tell when people are about to violate an act in the matter of discrimination when it's a word that hasn't even been defined in the bill? The word religion is not defined. The word race is not defined. National origin is not defined. Or creed, or color.

24

None of them are defined. It's all left to the discretion of those who enforce this act.

Speech
Earlham College
Richmond, Indiana
April 20, 1964

...Communist Endorsement. (The Civil Rights) bill has been endorsed and pushed by the *Communist Daily Worker* in every section of it and not a one of them believes man has a soul or has any after-life and doesn't believe that man is made in the image of God. Every left-wing organization in America who doesn't believe in the existence of God is behind this bill.

Speech
Earlham College
Richmond, Indiana
April 20, 1964

... Dictatorship. It is an ungarnished fact of truth that the official Communist Party of the United States is an enthusiastic supporter of the Civil Rights Bill. Well they might be, for this bill takes a long step toward transferring private property to public domain under a central government. It is this way in Russia. It places in the hands of a few men in central government the power to create a regulatory police arm unequaled in western civilization—power to investigate, to arrest, to charge and try a citizen without a jury of his peers—power to control the voting booth—power to invade private property without compensation or due process of law—power to enter every community, every business and level the American citizen to a common denominator called "equality" that is necessary for central planning and management of an entire people by government authority. And with this power, this bill hands over to a few men indiscriminate control of billions of dollars to use as they will—to intimidate, to withhold livelihood from those who would oppose their power, and to reward those who would aid in perpetuating that power. Under any name, it will create a dictatorship the like of which we or our fathers have not witnessed. It will bring about the ultimate in tyranny. It will make government master and god over man.

Speech
Whitewater State College
Wisconsin
March 23, 1964

. . . **Government Control.** There's concern about the government's attempt to regulate people's private lives and to take over the control of their homes, businesses, farms, labor unions and schools and local government bodies under the Civil Rights Bill. (The people) feel that you're really destroying the American concept of government when you do so.

Interview
U. S. News and
World Report
June 1, 1964

. . . They say imbalance in employment is discrimination. And this (Civil Rights) bill calls under FEPC Title Six for removal of discrimination because of race, creed, color or national origin. Under this bill, if a farmer, under Title Six, is drawing price supports or he's got a house or farm being bought under a federal program and he's got a Japanese Methodist working for him, a Chinese Baptist can come in and say I'd like to have this job because we've got some Chinese Americans living here. And if he doesn't give him a job, if he alleges discrimination, he puts the farmer in court, who has to prove that he hasn't discriminated because of religion or race. And therefore you are guilty under this bill until you are proven innocent. You're not innocent until you are proven guilty. And any man who loses a job under this bill or doesn't get a job he can allege discrimination and put the businessman in court right off . . . So, under this bill if they decide the farmer is discriminating because he's got all Japanese Baptists and has left the Chinese Methodists out, they'll order him to hire some Chinese Methodists and balance his work force and if he doesn't, they withdraw his price supports or whatever other federal program he's involved with. And I don't think the Federal Government ought to be telling a farmer in Indiana who he can work or who he can't work. I think he ought to be able to hire people with bald heads or barefooted folks if he wants to.

Speech
Earlham College
Richmond, Indiana
April 20, 1964

. . . As soon as this (Civil Rights) bill passes they're going to take the enforcement of your FEPC and public accommodations acts away from state folks and put it in the Federal Government. I feel that if you people want to have that law enforced on you, it ought to be enforced by local courts and local judges and local officials. The bill says that if you are effectively carrying out the provisions of

28

your act then all's well and good. You can continue to operate it. Who's going to decide whether you are effectively enforcing it or not? Under this bill the bureaucrats in Washington will decide that. And I don't think they ought to decide that. I don't think they ought to have a right to decide whether you are effectively enforcing this act or not.

Speech
Earlham College
Richmond, Indiana
April 20, 1964

. . . **Jury Trials.** Whenever the Government of the United States has a bill (Civil Rights) that gives it more power in one act than it has gotten in all the acts passed since this nation came into being, and will send a man to the penitentiary for violating it without a trial by jury then you have abolished the most basic of civil rights that exist in this country . . . One of the things that brought on the American revolution was the fact that the British crown deprived us of some of our liberty without benefit of trial by jury. And I think that a man is entitled to a jury trial, I don't care if it's going to take one minute . . . But this bill is not going to give a jury trial. It's an attack upon the jury system of this country. And whenever they can put your father, a businessman, or put your mother, in jail as boarding house or beauty shop operator or barber, in jail without a trial by jury then you're not going to have civil rights long because that's a basic civil right.

Speech
Earlham College
Richmond, Indiana
April 20, 1964

... **Labor Unions.** This (Civil Rights) bill affects labor unions probably as much as any other phase of activity. It says that you must end discrimination in the labor unions on the basis of race, color, creed or national origin. ... Under this bill if a labor union on the job got 100 Methodists, then a Baptist can come in and say . . . I've got seniority, you're discriminating because of religion and therefore that puts the labor unions and contractor . . . in the court and they can get them all tied up . . . Whenever you pass a bill that will tell a union that you've got 100 Japanese Methodists on the seniority list here and there are some Japanese Presbyterians who got to come on regardless of their seniority, and you take a job away from one man and give it to

30

another, you're not helping any problem, you're compounding a problem.

Speech
Earlham College
Richmond, Indiana
April 20, 1964

COERCION

... A crash program, as we are seeing in the Civil Rights Bill, always crashes. Forced mixing will only bring bitterness in any section. A voluntary program will eventually work itself out, but no one in a free government wants to be told what to do.

Radio Interview
January, 1966

COMMUNISM

... **Cause.** The liberals' theory that poverty, discrimination and lack of opportunity is the cause of communism is a false theory. If it were true the South would have been the biggest single Communist bloc in the Western Hemisphere long ago.

Inaugural Address
Montgomery, Alabama
January 14, 1963

... **States' Sovereignty.** We know by way of actual declaration that the leaders of world communism intend to attempt to destroy our political system. We know that our system under the Constitution guaranteeing the dissemination of power among the now 50 states, preventing a concentration of central authority, is a frustrating roadblock to communism and its liberal forerunners. Hence, we have witnessed a venomous attack on all who believe in states' sovereignty. We have witnessed a propaganda barrage of emotionalism that creates a climate of hysteria in promoting and justifying deliberate violations of those rights by judicial edict and physical force.

Speech
Whitewater State College
Wisconsin
March 23, 1964

COMMUNISTS

... Communists will take advantage of any unrest in America to foster their own goals.

Speech
University of Cincinnati
February 11, 1964

CONDESCENSION

... I don't want to be petted like a little poodle dog by a bunch of social engineers in Washington.

Column
Life Magazine
May 8, 1964

CONGRESS

... A Communist hates the Congress for the Congress is representative of the people. It is unwieldy. It is large. It has differing opinions— differing prejudices. It is rampant with debate and deliberation—and most important— with truths. Communism cannot survive where there is truth. A Communist applauds government by executive or judicial edict. A President can be forcibly removed and his authority easily assumed. A judiciary of only nine men may be deceived, or brainwashed, or corrupted. But a Congress represents the people and is directly responsible to the people—it represents the authority of the people.

Speech
Whitewater State College
Wisconsin
March 23, 1964

CONSERVATISM

... I'll sit on the right, Mr. President, and you may sit on the left.

> *Upon boarding the Presidential helicopter, when asked by President Kennedy where he would like to sit. The Wallace Story, by BILL JONES (Viewpoint Publications).*

... I'm not against progress. Conservatism doesn't mean being reactionary and not doing anything. It means progress but it means least governmental interference in unions, and labor and management, in business in schools and hospitals and all of those things.

> *Press Conference Greenville, S. C. July, 1967*

... When we build roads we conserve our industrial and business potential, which has increased our wealth many times over what we borrowed to build the roads. And the

34

schools were built to conserve the youth of
our state. That's conservatism.

Interview
U. S. News and
World Report
March 20, 1967

... "Conservatism" means to conserve that
which we consider to be good. I am a "conservative" in the sense that I am against governmental regulation.

Interview
U. S. News and
World Report
March 20, 1967

... **and Liberalism.** The definition of "conservatism" and "liberalism" has been all con-
fused. The true "liberals" in the past have
been those who did not want governmental
regimentation. It was the "liberals" in other
countries in years past who repealed restrictive laws against human liberties and individual freedoms. Now the "liberals" are the
ones in our country today who want to re-
strict individuals because they have no con-
fidence in them.

Interview
U. S. News and
World Report
March 20, 1967

CONSTITUTIONAL RIGHTS

. . . It is the right of every citizen, however humble he may be, through his chosen officials of representative government to stand courageously against whatever he believes to be the exercise of power beyond the constitutional rights conferred upon our Federal Government.

> *"School House Door"*
> *Speech*
> *University of Alabama*
> *June 11, 1963*

. . . **Religion.** We don't like some of the trends going on in the country. I resent and reject the trend when your federal court system has ruled for the first time that the reading of a simple Bible reading with no comment in a public school is unlawful and unconstitutional. The saying of a simple prayer in a public school system in our country today is unlawful and unconstitutional. And when Chief Justice Earl Warren of the Supreme Court of the United States refuses, at the request of the Congress to put the words: "In God We Trust" above the bench of his court, because he says that violates the

Constitution of the United States, I don't ac-
cept those trends, I reject them.

Speech
Earlham College
Richmond, Indiana
April 20, 1964

CORRUPTION

... There has been an erosion of integrity
among many of the leaders of the country as
evidenced by the five-percenters, those who
want to make an easy buck, the grafters and
chislers who want 'a living' without working.
This erosion of integrity has reached the level
of state government in many instances . . .
Every dollar wasted on political payoffs in
Alabama takes a dollar away from the old
people, the school children, the blind and
mentally ill and causes the people to lose
faith in state government, and this is the
greatest curse of it all. I shall not use the
office of governor to make me and my family
or political cronies rich. Incorruptible state
government will be our source of strength in
the future, for the people will follow such

leadership in settling the problems of the day.

*Meeting of Montgomery
County
Wallace-for-Governor
Volunteers
January 22, 1962*

COURT ORDERS

. . . I will do whatever a court order issued tells me to do. I may not like the court order, but I can tell you this, that we have always obeyed court orders, and we will obey the next court order, and we also expect other people to obey court orders . . . I don't like federal court orders. I don't like what the federal courts have done to this country, and I am going to work to change things that have happened in our country which I think are not in the interest of any citizen.

*Press Conference
Montgomery, Alabama
March 14, 1965*

COURTS

. . . The courts are institutions designed by man. They are not divine . . . You have a right to criticize the governor of a state; under academic freedom and freedom of speech you can criticize the President; why can you not criticize the separate branch of the government called the Judiciary which is on an equal scale with that of the Executive, supposedly?

Speech
Rose Polytechnic
Institute
Terre Haute, Indiana
Spring, 1967

... **Contracts**. It had long ·been a settled principle of law that under our Constitution private individuals could enter into contracts respecting control and disposition of their own property as they saw fit so long as it did not harm another; that contracts containing restrictive covenants as to the use of private property were valid, that persons buying a home could select their future neighbors. No act of Congress was passed, no amendment of the Constitution was adopted, yet after a fine day in the spring of 1948, this fundamental principle of law was swept aside. This (Supreme) Court, with political causes to serve, held that while such contracts were legal, the courts of the land could not enforce them—hence they were futile and useless.

Speech
Harvard University
November, 1963

... **Judicial Oligarchy**. The fact that the American people must petition Congress for a restoration of their basic rights to worship God in the manner and in the places they see fit should be a red signal of danger flashing a warning to the extent to which we have become subordinated to government. We are being manipulated by the courts as cogs in a gigantic socialistic pattern in which the federal judiciary amends the Constitution, establishes public policy, initiates and administers social reform and decrees for the people every aspect and element of their personal lives, all of which is devoid of the concept of God. The responsibility for this disgraceful situation must be shared by those members of the United States Congress who have failed to rise to the dignity of their station by acting to check the head-long rush toward destruction of our system as established by the Founding Fathers. The responsibility must be shared by those members of the Congress who have failed to regulate but instead have rubberstamped a judicial oligarchy~in its most malignant form. The responsibility must be shared by those members of the Congress who today sponsor legislation which takes power from the people and lodges it in an autocratic central government. This responsibility must be shared by those members of the United States Senate who have confirmed the appointment of persons ill-equipped in law and who admittedly possess no special competence to adjudicate the Constitution of the United States as written. Until appointments of the highest court of the land are made on the basis of judicial ability, and not on the basis of politics, there can be no assurance that our governmental system will endure.

> *Testimony Before the*
> *House Judiciary*
> *Committee*
> *April* 21, 1964

CRIME

... I'm not against probation; I was the first judge in our circuit to make use of probation. And I certainly believe in seeing that a defendant gets all the rights he has coming to him. But the people have rights too. I'd take one of our fine members of the Supreme Court of Alabama and make him Chief Justice of the United States, and by God you'd see some changes made.

*Interview with James
Jackson Kilpatrick
National Review
April 18, 1967*

. . . We have a system today in our country by which course law and order has broken down . . . Crime has risen in our country at an astronomical rate and the court system now has ruled that you can hardly convict a criminal. If you are knocked in the head on a street in a city today, the man who knocked you in the head is out of jail before you get to the hospital, much less out of the hospital. And they can't tell me that we can't adopt a system in this country that will protect the individual liberties and freedoms of our people and at the same time incarcerate a man who is a self-confessed murderer of five or more people. That system is not a good system.

*Speech
Terre Haute, Indiana
Spring, 1967*

. . . Completely irresponsible court action is

favoring those who do not wish to follow
the law.

Press Conference
Greenville, S. C.
July 19, 1967

... The reason why we have so much crime
in our country is that we have a system of
courts that tries to play God.

New York Times
April 29, 1967

... **Punishment.** Supreme Court decisions
have made it almost impossible for police
to arrest a criminal. Politicians are always
trying to explain why some people don't obey
the law—because they didn't have any water-
melon when they were small children. Then
when theoreticians try to explain why somebody hits you with a brick, but if these people
knew punishment by law would be swift
and sure, they wouldn't hit you with a brick.

Press Conference
July 19, 1967

... **Responsibility.** The leadership of both
national parties are responsible for it not
being safe on our streets.

Speech
August 9, 1967

··D··

DEMOCRATS

... I am an Alabama Democrat, not a national Democrat. I'm not kin to those folks. The difference between a national Democrat and an Alabama Democrat is like the difference between a Communist and a non-Communist.

*New York Times
Magazine
April 24, 1966*

DEMONSTRATIONS

Pickets have a right to picket. Peaceful picketing is part of the American system; peaceful demonstrations are a part of the American system.

*Interview
Face the Nation
(CBS-TV)
March 14, 1965*

... I have always told the state police that

44

they must use only the minimum force necessary to handle demonstrations or marches.

Reply to a Petition
Presented to the
Governor After the
Selma-to
Montgomery
Civil Rights March
March 30, 1965

... There must be a cessation of these
(racial) demonstrations throughout the country, or it is going to take the federal, state,
local and county police to protect the consi-
tutional rights of the non-demonstrators in
this country, because, after all, the safety of
the people upon the street is threatened by
continuous demonstrations, day in and day
out.

Interview
Face the Nation
(CBS-TV)
March 14, 1965

... I think that when demonstrations get to
the point that they interfere with the rights of
others, then in my judgement, they cease to
become peaceful. And I might point out
that many peaceful demonstrations by Negro
citizens of this state have been carried out

45

throughout Alabama . . . And we have lent support to them in that we have had policemen there to see that no one got hurt in the demonstrations. I am for peaceful demonstrations but I don't think that peaceful demonstrations should run eight long weeks.

Interview
Face the Nation
(CBS-TV)
March 14, 1965

. . . We see today a foreign philosophy that says to the people, "You need not bother to work and meet the qualifications of a free man. All you must do is demonstrate and cause chaos and create a situation whereby our propagandists, masquerading as newsmen, may destroy faith in local law enforcement and impugn the decency of local law enforcement so that we may take all police powers unto the central government." That is the ominous price that the irresponsible demonstrators pay—many of them Communist-trained—to bring about such a development.

Address
Joint Session of the
*   Alabama Legislature*
Montgomery, Alabama
March 18, 1965

DISCRIMINATION

... Under Title Six (of the Civil Rights Bill) every agency that has anything to do with federal forms or any federal programs is called upon to remove discrimination in the matter of employment and otherwise. Now what is discrimination? It ought to be defined. A bureaucrat in Washington will say discrimination is one thing and you will say it's another.

Speech
Earlham College
Richmond, Indiana
April 20, 1964

DISSENT

... I believe in the right of dissent. I believe you have the right to speak your mind.

Speech
Rose Polytechnic
Institute
Terre Haute, Indiana
Spring, 1967

... and Treason. There are honest conscientious, loyal Americans including some members of the Congress, who dissent about our position in Vietnam. But dissent is being abused when some college professor or so-called pacifist says he longs for a victory of the Viet Cong over the American "imperialist" servicemen. And dissent is abused when money, clothes, and blood are raised for the Viet Cong. These people are not dissenters, but instead, they are guilty of treason. I would have the Justice Department attempt to indict such people and bring them to trial in the proper courts for treason.

Newsweek
July 10, 1967

··E··

EDUCATION

... Education is really the solution to the problems that face the people of every state in the Union.

Speech
Earlham College
Richmond, Indiana
April 20, 1964

... No one who finishes high school or technical school or goes to college has any problems finding his way in the American economy. It is those of all races and colors who drop out in the third or fourth grade and then ten or 15 years later expect to have an income similar to that of those who have finished their education. So education does provide and will provide the solution not only to economic problems of families but also to social problems that confront peoples of our country and the various and sundry states.

Speech
Rose Polytechnic
Institute
Spring, 1967

...I want to assure every child that this state government is not afraid to invest in their future through education, so that they will not be handicapped on the very threshhold of their lives.

Inaugural Address
Montgomery, Alabama
January 14, 1963

...**Dropouts.** Drop-outs are the main problem we have in Alabama in educating members of the Negro race. This problem must be solved. We have to keep these people in school, because if they drop out of school in the second, third or fourth grade, then ten years later, they can't get a job because they are not trained for any type of job, and thus they must get on relief to have money for food. This is the main reason why I am working for a free text book program, because studies have shown that one of the major reasons for dropouts is the lack of books in order for each student to keep up with the studies.

*Reply to Petition
Presented to the
Governor After the
Selma-to-Montgomery
Civil Rights March
March* 30, 1965

...Negro. While I was in the legislature of my state, I sponsored the bill that built the largest Negro trade school in the South and I made their dedication speeches and their graduation addresses. And I have served for two years on the board of trustees of the most renowned Negro college in the world, Tuskegee Institute.

*Speech
Earlham College
Richmond, Indiana
April* 20, 1964

...South. To ask us to equate our children, classroom for classroom, with a race that is two years behind at the sixth grade and three years behind at the twelfth grade is to ask us to deprive our children of the education to which they are entitled and, in the effort to give this, we strain our resources to the utmost. It is our problem, not yours. Your

51

problem here is yours, not ours. We ask you to believe that we are civilized, humane and considerate of human rights. We give you the credit for so being and we ask you to extend us the same consideration.

Speech
Harvard University
November 11, 1963

ELECTIONS

... **Plurality.** Lincoln was a plurality winner. In a four-party race, Lincoln did not get a majority of the popular votes, but he got a majority of electoral votes.

Interview
March 20, 1967

· · F · ·

FASCISM

... **vs. Communism.** I'd rather be a Fascist than a Communist. At least a Fascist believes in God!

> *New York Times*
> *Magazine*
> *April 24, 1966*

FEDERAL AID

... I'm not against federal aid to education for the simple reason that this is not Federal aid, it's tax money from the pockets of South Carolinians and Alabamians and Mississippians . . . You can't be against it because they've got all the money up there (In Washington). If you didn't get some of that money back then you wouldn't have a school system in South Carolina, or a road system. I would ask them to reduce taxes from the American people and then let the states themselves decide whether they wanted to recoup those taxes through local taxation. I'm against federal controls of the school system. But just because they give the South Carolina people some of their own money back doesn't give them any right to then say, we are going to determine everything about your school child ourselves. Why, just because you get some of your own money back, they are going to say now we are going to run the school system? That's what we're opposed to.

Press Conference
Greenville, S. C.
July, 1967

. . . I'm not against taking federal aid because there's no such thing really as federal aid. Federal aid, so-called, is tax payers' money paid by the tax payers to the Federal Government. And if the people did not get some of their own money back for their schools and roads, then you would have to raise taxes prohibitively upon the people locally. I'm against federal controls, and as President, if I were a candidate and if I were elected, I would get out of the control of the school system. I wouldn't end federal aid, so-called, because that cannot be done abruptly. But gradually we could reduce taxes on the federal level and then let the states, if they saw fit, recoup in local taxes.

Press Conference
Greenville, S. C.
July, 1967

... We don't get any federal aid, because there is no such thing. It is taxpayers' aid, because it is your money and my money, and they just return a small portion to us after throwing most of it down a rat hole somewhere.

Press Conference
Terre Haute, Indiana
1964 *Presidential*
Primary Campaign

FEDERAL GOVERNMENT

... I'm not fighting the Federal Government; I'm fighting this outlaw beatnik crowd in Washington that has just about destroyed the Federal Government, and I'm trying to save it.

New York Times
Magazine
April 24, 1966

... It's immoral for the Federal Government to destroy the local government of the State of Indiana—or any other state. It's immoral for the Federal Government to take over every farm and business and home and labor union and school in this state away from local control.

Speech
Earlham College
Richmond, Indiana
April 20, 1964

FEDERAL-STATE RELATIONS

... (If I were President today) my general philosophy in the area of federal-state relations would be that which the Constitution provides. That is, those powers not delegated to the Federal Government are reserved to the people. Insofar as domestic institutions are concerned, such as for instance the schools which is a prime example of the complete take-over by the Federal Government, I would place the Health, Education, Welfare Department in its place, I would take them out of the hair of the education officials of the states, and I would work toward complete restoration of the right of the people of the respective states to determine the policies of local democratic institutions.

Press Conference
Greenville, S. C.
July, 1967

FEDERAL vs. STATE GOVERNMENT

... My administration will support all federal programs in Alabama that promote the best interests of the people of Alabama, but by the same token, the Wallace administration will firmly resist dictation and control by federal agencies in areas which traditionally and constitutionally are matters for state and local control. Our way of life can and must be preserved.

Speech
Campaign for Governor
of Alabama
1962

FOREIGN AID

... I'm sick of billions of dollars wasted in foreign countries when many of those countries ship materials to Vietnam to help kill American servicemen.

Press Conference
Greenville, S. C.
July 19, 1967

... We ought to re-evaluate our entire foreign aid program insofar as some of the money we spend because lots of it is being wasted. Lots

57

of it is going down a rat hole and I'm tired
of money going down rat holes.

Speech
Earlham College
Richmond, Indiana
April 20, 1964

FOREIGN AID vs. DOMESTIC PROGRAMS

. . . The "liberals" are always saying we must
give foreign aid throughout the world without any strings attached. But then when they
give you your own tax money back in this
country they say it's got to have every string
attached under the sun.

Interview
U. S. News and
World Report
March 20, 1967

FOREIGN AFFAIRS

. . . I have no experience in (foreign affairs),
but you all know what the country is like
now. It got that way through experience. What
we need in Washington, now is a little in-
experience.

Speech
Indiana University
April 23, 1964

FOREIGN POLICY

. . . The United States hasn't had much of a foreign policy for a number of years and no one in Washington knows what it is either. We talk about a blockade of Cuba, but at the same time the United States is selling wheat to Russia!

> *Press Conference*
> *Appleton, Wisconsin*
> *1964 Presidential*
> *Primary Campaign*

. . . The American taxpayer is now financing food for the Russians in order to ease their internal pressure. We might propose to cut off that wheat. We might arm the underground patriots of Cuba, furnishing the necessary air cover. We might then offer troops to any South American government requesting them, to mop up the saboteurs, the fifth columnists, the rioters and the Communist-trained street fighters. We might call together the Western nations of the world with the rededication of principle instead of betrayal and bring economic and political pressures to bear to negotiate freedom for our valiant allies in Poland, Hungary, Czechoslovakia, East Germany and other nations. We are feeding and supporting half the Communist nations of the world at this moment. What is our return? Let us re-evaluate our position.

Speech
Whitewater State College
Wisconsin
March 23, 1964

FREEDOM

. . . As free men we do not recognize any government right to give freedom, or deny freedom. No government erected by man has that right.

Inaugural Address
Montgomery, Alabama
January 14, 1963

FREEDOM OF SPEECH

. . . Freedom of speech is part of the American system. But as the President himself said, it doesn't give you the right to go into a crowded theater and holler "fire."

Interview
Face the Nation
(CBS-TV)
March 14, 1965

FREE ENTERPRISE SYSTEM

... I'm sick of attacks on the free enterprise system.

Press Conference
Greenville, S. C.
July 19, 1967

... Private property and the free enterprise system are under attack by the liberal-Socialist-Communist crowd.

N. Y. Times Magazine
April 24, 1966

··G··

GOD

... We, in our part of the country, are old-fashioned. We still believe there is a God. In the liberal circles, you know, they believe their minds are the greatest things in the universe. We don't think so in Alabama. We think, and know, there is a God Who made all of us and that He loves all of us, even though it is old-fashioned now.

Speech
Earlham College
Richmond, Indiana
April 20, 1964

... **Eternity.** The human mind cannot comprehend that which has no beginning or end (eternity). Yet, God encompasses eternity, and man can comprehend God to the extent that God grants the capability. To that extent I understand eternity to be shaped by God's will.

Christian Century
April 21, 1965

GOVERNMENT

... **All-Powerful.** We can no longer hide our head in the sand and tell ourselves that the ideology of our forefathers is not being attacked and is not being threatened by another idea ... for it is. We are faced with an idea that if a centralized government assumes enough authority, enough power over its people, that it can provide a utopian life. ... That if given the power to dictate, to forbid, to require, to demand, to distribute, to edict and to judge what is best and enforce the will of judgment upon its citizens from unimpeachable authority ... then it will produce only "good" ... and it shall be our father ... and our God. It is an idea of government that encourages our fears and destroys our faith ... for where there is faith, there is no fear, and where there is fear, there is no faith.

Inaugural Address
Montgomery, Alabama
January 14, 1963

... **Federal vs. State.** Race should not be an issue in our (Presidential) campaign at all. The issue will be whether or not the government of the United States can take over and destroy the authority of the States—whether it be Alabama or New York or any other State.

Interview
U. S. News and
World Report
March 20, 1967

...**Force.** You don't solve any problem by more federal force, the government forcing you to do something. It makes you a government-fearing folk instead of a God-fearing people.

Speech
Earlham College
Richmond, Indiana
April 20, 1964

...**vs. God.** We are beginning to be a Government-fearing instead of a God-fearing people.

Interview
U. S. News and
World Report
April 20, 1964

GOVERNMENT CONTROL

...I object to no one being employed because of their race, creed or color or national origin but I object to the Federal Government

64

telling farmers what they can and what they cannot do.

Speech
Earlham College
Richmond, Indiana
April 20, 1964

... There is a new trend in this country. There is a heavy undercurrent of resentment among the mass of the people toward the solution of all problems with more federal force and more take-over of individual liberty and freedom.

Interview
U. S. News and
World Report
June 1, 1964

... The average citizens who make this country hum and keep her moving are sick and tired of theoreticians in both national parties and in some of our colleges and some of our courts telling us how to go to bed at night and get up in the morning. So what I'm trying to say is that no candidate (for the Presidency in 1968) would be acceptable to me unless he and the platform said specifically among other things—that he is going to turn back to the people of South Carolina and all other states the right to determine the policies of the education of their children.

Press Conference
Greenville, S. C.
July, 1967

GOVERNMENT INTERFERENCE

. . . By the fall of 1968, the people in Cleveland and Chicago and Gary and St. Louis will be so sick and tired of federal interference in their local schools, they'll be ready to vote for Wallace by the thousands. The people don't like this trifling with their children, telling them which teachers have to teach in which schools, and bussing little boys and girls half across a city just to achieve "the proper racial mix." That's no business of the Federal Government! Where do they find authority for that in the Constitution? Education isn't mentioned in the Constitution.

Interview with
James Jackson Kilpatrick
National Review
April 18, 1967

. . . It's not the business of government to tell a businessman how to run his business.

To President Kennedy
May 13, 1963

66

. . . Any time the Federal Government tries to lay down the law for people all over this country, fixing the terms and conditions on which they can sell their homes, the Federal Government is going to have resistence on its hands. And not just in the South. Everywhere. Folks won't stand for it. And there's nothing about the sale of private housing in the Constitution either.

Interview with
James Jackson Kilpatrick
National Review
April 18, 1967

. . . If I were President of the United States I would stop these Washington bureaucrats from trying to tell New York or California or Alabama or Georgia or any other State how to run the schools. I'd jerk them out of that business so fast they wouldn't know what happened—and I'd jerk them out of the hospital business and I'd jerk them out of interfering with labor unions, and I'd jerk them out of interfering with people's business.

Interview
U. S. News and
World Report
March 20, 1967

... They (the Federal Government) use a race issue to come in and take over hospitals, to take over the control of textbooks. They say we've got distorted textbooks. So they're using that issue to try to determine what little children shall be taught, what they shall learn. And I believe that when this is fully explained to people of all races in this country they are going to be against big government running their lives.

Interview
U. S. News and
World Report
March 20, 1967

... The "liberals" and the so-called intellectuals—intellectual morons—have always tried to make racists out of us who have opposed governmental interference in local democratic institutions, because logically they can't argue with the theory that people in New York and California and Alabama and Ohio can best determine what is in the best interest of our own children.

Interview
U. S. News and
World Report
March 20, 1967

... Isn't it strange how they give our money to all those countries and don't even question their local customs? But right here in our own country they want to change the customs of a sovereign state. Over in Africa, they've got a local custom of eating each other.

N. Y. Times Magazine
April 24, 1966

GOVERNMENT MANAGEMENT

... The world is at war between two ideals of government. I am here because I believe we can no longer comfortably contemplate that war from afar. There is the ideal that believes government can manage the people and, by management and manipulations, bring about a utopian life. This ideal has come to be a predominant aim in Washington.

Speech
Whitewater State College
Wisconsin
March 23, 1964

GOVERNMENT SPENDING

... They (the Federal Government) spend $6 million to put one Negro in Ole Miss and it could have been spent for training Negro children in Mississippi. But if that kind of money goes to Rangoon or Ghana, and the schools are segregated, what difference does that make?

Press Conference
Columbus, Ohio
February 12, 1964

GOVERNORSHIP

... Both (my wife and I) of us will be the Governor of this state (Alabama). I will make the policy decisions during her term of office.

Time Magazine
March 4, 1966

... I would see any group of Alabamians who came to see me, because I am the Governor of all the people of this state, and I have never declined to see anybody because of their race, color, creed, religion or national origin. I have seen Negro school children come through my office to see the Governor of their state and I have given them pictures and I have signed autographs for them, and I will do it again, because I am the Governor of all the people of Alabama.

Interview
Face the Nation
(*CBS-TV*)
March 14, 1965

GUILT-BY-ASSOCIATION

... You can't equate a candidate with everyone who supports him. In the 1964 election, the *Communist Daily Worker* endorsed President Johnson and many of his policies. But I would be the last man to say the President is a Communist. He's not a Communist. He's anti-Communist.

Press Conference
Greenville, South Carolina
July 19, 1967

GUN LAW

... (A federal gun law will) keep guns out of the hands of law-abiding citizens and those who break the law will have them anyway.

Interview with
Vera Glaser
North American
Newspaper Alliance
August 28, 1967

71

·· H ··

HARVARD

... **Intellectuals.** I spoke at the long-haired ✓
college of Harvard; I told them we got people
in Alabama as intelligent and refined and
cultured as you are and don't you ever for-
get it. I made the best speech they ever heard
up at Harvard and, you know, the next day
hundreds of them got their hair cut.

Newsweek
May 19, 1966

HATE

... I advocate hatred of no man, because
hate will only compound the problems facing
the South.

Opening Speech
1958 Campaign for
Governor of Alabama

... Much has been written and said about
the "hate" that is purportedly present in our
society. Much has been written and said about

72

the "haters." Invariably those who are identified as the purveyors of hate are:

Those who believe in the rights of the individual states.

Those who believe in fiscal responsibility.

Those who object to amendment of the Constitution of the United States without regard to the basic precepts of the founding fathers.

Those who stand firm for the retention of the checks and balances system of government.

Those who object to a socialist ideology under which a few men in the executive and judicial branches of our government make decisions and laws without regard to our elected representatives who reflect the decisions of the people.

Speech
Whitewater State College
Wisconsin
March 14, 1965

HOSPITALS

... **Racial Equality.** No Negro has ever been turned away from any hospital in Alabama because he is a Negro, and if any ever

73

are turned away that I find out about I will
put a stop to it.

Interview
Face the Nation
(CBS-TV)
March 19, 1965

HYPOCRISY

... Northern hypocrisy is a problem that
must be contended with. What is termed a
race riot in the South is called civil disobedi-
ence in New York or Chicago. Take, for
example, integration in Washington, D. C.,
which is supposed to be the personification
of what is good. In Alabama we don't take
what Washington does as divine—when Washington schools integrated, the proportion of
white in the schools was high. Now the proportion of Negroes there is high and all the
whites are taking children to Virginia and
Maryland. In fact, I flew over Washington
last week and saw they are building a new
bridge over the Potomac—for all the white
liberals fleeing to Virginia.

Speech
Notre Dame University
South Bend, Indiana
April 29, 1964

... Much of the hate and bitterness and
ill-will in the country is engendered by gov-

ernment hypocrites who preach one thing and practice another.

Meeting with
Protestant Ministers
Oshkosh, Wisconsin
April, 1964

. . . We in Alabama have been forthright in our position. But these officials in Washington who are always prodding about desegregation and integration are the same folks who move their children to Virginia and Maryland where they've really got a segregated school system. I resent that hypocrisy. The Negro citizens of this country, in my judgement, are going to come to see that this hypocrisy has not been in their interests and never will be.

Interview
U. S. News and
World Report
March 20, 1967

$$\bullet \ \bullet \ \text{I} \ \bullet \ \bullet$$

IMPARTIALITY

... I have never made a derogatory remark about one of God's children and I never will. If I am elected, I am going to treat all fairly.

Interview
March 20, 1967

INDIVIDUAL FREEDOM

... You don't solve problems by passing legislation that restricts individual freedom and free enterprise.

Speech
Cambridge, Maryland
1964 Presidential
Primary Campaign

INDUSTRY

... **Alabama.** We are committed during this administration to the progress and expansion of industry because this creates jobs for all

Alabamians, giving each an opportunity to provide a better way of life for himself and his family. Our attitude on industry is best gauged by our recognition that profits are the key to continued industrial growth. We are dedicated to and believe in the free enterprise system. Alabamians want state industries to operate profitably—to gain a full measure of success, for industry means jobs for our citizens. Industry is welcome in Alabama.

Speech
Recognition Ceremony
  for One Billion Dollars
  of Industrial Growth
July, 1965

INTEGRATION

. . . Integration is a matter to be decided by each state. The states must determine if they feel it is of benefit to both races.

Press Conference
Indianapolis, Indiana
1964 *Presidential*
  Primary Campaign

INTEGRITY

. . . In the long run, doing the right and honorable thing is the best politics, but even

if it isn't we are still going to do the right
thing.

Quoted by Bill Jones
The Wallace Story
(Viewpoint Publications)

INTELLECT

...vs. God. I'm not like all these pseudo-
liberals who think that their mind is the greatest thing on earth. I believe that God made
us all and that He loves us all.

Speech
Indiana University
Bloomington, Indiana
April 23, 1964

INTELLECTUAL MORONS

... The people are going to be fed up with
the sissy attitude of Lyndon Johnson and all
the intellectual morons and theoreticians he
has around him. They're fed up with a Supreme
Court that—with a few exceptions—is a sorry,
lousy no-account outfit. Now, I don't mean
anything against the President personally, or
against the Court. I'm sure they're fine gentle-
men and I don't doubt they're sincere. But
they've been taken over by the intellectual
morons. You can see what's happened: mur-

der, rape, assault; and the criminals just laugh-
ing while the police are crying for help.

Interview with
James Jackson Kilpatrick
National Review
April 18, 1967

INTERNATIONALISM

... We should not do anything unilaterally
in (the Middle East) any more than we should
do anything else anyplace else   unilaterally.
We should do it bilaterally or multilaterally,
with the big powers.

Press Conference
Greenville, S. C.
July, 1967

INTERNATIONAL RELATIONS

... I believe in negotiating and talking across
the conference table. I believe that. But
I don't believe in sitting at every conference
table and getting out-maneuvered, and giving
something and never getting anything in return.

Press Conference
Greenville, S. C.
July, 1967

. . . I wouldn't build any bridge with anyone until they built part of the bridge themselves. And I would not trade with any
nation—I would not advocate trading with
nations that do business with those North
Vietnamese who are now killing American
servicemen. And I would also talk very straight
to our British allies who are good folks, but
they are trading with Cuba and North Vietnam
and we ought to look them straight in the
eye. And we ought to tell Mr. DeGaulle that
when you have balance of payments due you
in our gold, we're not going to let you drain
our gold supply and weaken the American
dollar which you are trying to do, we're
going to just cancel some of those dollars of
war debts that they owe us.

Press Conference
Greenville,
South Carolina
July, 1967

INTERPOSITION

. . . I shall react vigorously to outside med-
dling. We shall fight the federals in the arena
of an increasingly sympathetic national public
opinion. We shall fight them in the arena of
our courts by interposing constitutional ques-
tions involving the sovereignty of this state

and the constitutional prerogatives of its chief executive. I pledge to stand between you and the efforts of a "force cult" to impose on you doctrines foreign to the concepts of our constitutional government, foreign to our way of life and disruptive of the peace and tranquility of our citizens. I will face our enemies face to face, hip to hip, and toe to toe, and never surrender your Governor's office to these carpetbaggers, scalawags and pollywogs. Right will prevail if we fight. We can have peace and progress in Alabama if we stand firm. There is no other way.

> *Plan of Progress*
> *Election Brochure*
> 1962 *Campaign for*
> *Governor of Alabama*

INTERRACIAL MARRIAGE

... I don't think interracial marriage is good for either race and I am against it.

> *Meeting with*
> *Protestant Ministers*
> *Oshkosh, Wisconsin*
> *April,* 1964

• • J • •

JOB DISTRIBUTION

. . . If you are a farmer employing Japanese Methodists, this (Civil Rights) bill can force you to hire some Chinese Baptists, because the bill says you can't discriminate because of race, religion, or national origin. The bill will not help labor, because it does not create one single job. All it does is take your job and give it to someone else.

JUDGES

. . . We are sick and tired of federal judges playing God on the court benches.
. . . I want an independent judiciary, but one made up of men who know the Constitution and have a little experience.
. . . We don't like federal judges running our local democratic institutions.

JUDICIAL POWER

. . . **Misuse.** It is fantastic that the American people find it necessary to beseech the Congress for the restoration of our cherished right to permit our children to participate in a simple invocation at the beginning of a school day in our neighborhood schools. That right has been nullified by the United States Supreme Court by a decree as sweeping and as deadly as any ever issued by any dictatorial power on the face of this earth. This decision is part and parcel of the judicial philosophy that has transformed limitations of power upon the Federal Government. It is the bitter fruit of the liberal dogma that worships human intelligence and scorns the concept of Divinity. It is part of the philosophy of socialism elevated to the diginity of law by decisions of the Court in which the concept of private property is under continuous attack. It is part of the deliberate design to subordinate the American people, their faith, their customs and their religious traditions to a Godless state. The federal judiciary has made a hollow mockery of the guarantees of the Bill of Rights. It has sounded the death knell to the democratic institution of local schools controlled by local elected school officials. It is an ironic paradox that the trustees of our liberties should become the oppressors of the people. When the crimes of humanity are finally catalogued, this monstrous breach of faith by the non-elected branch of the Federal Government must stand out as one of history's great infamies.

Testimony before the House Judiciary Committee on a Proposed Constitutional Amendment Guaranteeing Freedom of Worship
Washington, D. C.
April 21, 1963

JUDICIARY

... Thomas Jefferson is the man who long ago said the dissolution of the American Republic would come, if it does come, by an irresponsible federal judiciary, taking a little bit of power by night until it's all lodged in Washington.

Speech
Rose Polytechnic Institute
Terre Haute, Indiana
Spring, 1967

... There is today a judicial dictatorship and judicial tyranny, unlike anything the nation has ever seen.

Speech
1962 Campaign for Governor of Alabama

84

... Nobody has ever questioned the power and right of the judiciary to be the interpreter and the adjudicator and to render decisions on ambiguous portions of legislative acts nor constitutional amendments. But it was always understood from the inception of our government that the judiciary would use restraint—judicial restraint—and would not usurp its authority, which it has done.

Speech
Earlham College
Richmond, Indiana
April 20, 1964

·· K ··

KU KLUX KLAN

... I am not a Klansman and haven't attend-
ed any Klan rallies.

Press Conference
Greenville,
*   South Carolina*
July 19, 1967

·· L ··

LAW

... What is law but the crystallization of
public opinion? For 100 years our laws,
segregation laws, have reflected the opinion

of the people of this state, and the Federal
Supreme Court upheld them all that time. Now
they want to come along and change them.
They didn't ask us, didn't care about our
opinion, didn't give a thought to the separate
schools we built with their blessing. They say
my defiance of federal law caused the climate
that led to the bombings. Martin Luther
King was the one who started breaking our
laws in Alabama. Why don't they blame him?
He broke our laws, but he says he doesn't
have to obey them because they're unjust.
Well, for 100 years the Supreme Court thought
they were just, and we still think so. And I
say the 1954 Supreme Court decision is the
most unjust law on the books.

N. Y. Times Magazine
April 24, 1966

. . . **Federal vs. Local.** The federal courts
have held in the last few years in the Communist cases and other cases that once the
Federal Government passes a law on a subject,
it takes away the right of the state then to
pass a law on the same subject. It has pre-
empted the field. In the Steve Nelson case,
36 states had laws that you could convict a
Communist for advocating overthrow of the
government by force and violence, so they

convicted Steve Nelson in Pennsylvania, a Communist. It got down to the Supreme Court and what did they say? No you can't convict him in Pennsylvania because if the federal government passes a law on the same subject, that takes over, pre-empts the field.

Speech
Earlham College
Richmond, Indiana
April 20, 1964

LAW AND ORDER

...I am for maintenance of law and order and desire to prevent violence and keep the peace.

Telegram to Pres. John
F. Kennedy
May 12, 1963

LAW ENFORCEMENT

...You can't arrest a Communist because of Supreme Court rulings and you can't walk the streets of large cities without fear of being hit over the head because the criminal would be let out of jail before you even got to the hospital.

Press Conference
Greenville,
South Carolina
July 19, 1967

88

...Any law passed by the American Congress and held constitutional will have to be enforced in this state (Alabama). We may not like it, and we will do our best to see that they are repealed, as we are going to work towards a repeal of the Civil Rights Bill, a modification of it, but we will have to abide by any law passed. We don't ask for defiance and anarchy.

Interview
Face the Nation
(CBS-TV)
March 14, 1965

...You can tell the Attorney General of the United States that, rather than go around attacking the individual rights of schoolchildren, he could spend his time better prosecuting these people who burn the country down and preach violence and overthrow of the government.

Associated Press
September 6, 1967

LAWLESSNESS

...Today a good citizen, regardless of his race, cannot walk safely in the streets and parks of many of the large cities of our country, because the court system of our country has made it impossible to convict a criminal.

Interview
U. S. News and
World Report
March 20, 1967

LAWS

... They keep passing laws on top of laws to favor persons who don't abide by laws.

Press Conference
Greenville, S. C.
July 19, 1967

LIBERAL REVOLUTION

... The person, whether he be a public official or an individual citizen, who attempts to stand in some manner of opposition to . . . (the) train of liberal revolution can virtually be destroyed by a flailing thresher of propaganda that smears him with a wide range of deprecating adjectives which can deceive and mislead the American public. This emotional wave of propaganda serves a purpose of silencing opposition and of creating an atmosphere of charged emotionalism in which factual knowledge goes by the board. I am alarmed and I believe the responsible citizens of America are alarmed.

Speech
Whitewater State College
Wisconsin
March 23, 1964

LIBERALS

... The international racism of the liberals seeks to persecute the international white minority to the whim of the international colored . . . so that we are footballed about according to the favor of the Afro-Asian bloc.

Inaugural Address
Montgomery, Alabama
January 14, 1963

LOCAL CONTROL

... You are intelligent enough to run your schools . . . If you are not intelligent enough to run your schools, you'd do just as well to do away with the city government of every city in the state and do away with your state capitol, because if the so-called Civil Rights Bill passes, you won't have any need for these functions of local government anyway. The people who hold office will have titles merely and you will have transposed all authority and power to Washington, D. C.

Speech
Earlham College
Richmond, Indiana
April 20, 1964

LOCAL GOVERNMENT

... The breakdown of local government will destroy the rights and liberties of all people regardless of their race or color.

Speech
Rose Polytechnic Institute
Terre Haute, Indiana
Spring, 1967

... I don't think that a government thousands of miles away can run the city's business better than the city's or state's elected officials.

Meeting with
*   Protestant Ministers*
Oshkosh, Wisconsin
April, 1964

... I'm sick and tired of seeing local institutions destroyed by the Federal Government.

> *Press Conference*
> *Greenville,*
> *   South Carolina*
> *July* 19, 1967

. . . We will awaken the nation to the liberal-Socialist-Communist design to destroy local government in America.

> *New York*
> *   Times Magazine*
> *April* 24, 1966

. . . When you destroy local government and transpose that authority and power to Washington you have destroyed the individual freedom and liberty of all the people within your state, regardless of their color, creed, race or national origin.

> *Speech*
> *Earlham College*
> *Richmond, Indiana*
> *April* 20, 1964

· · M · ·

MASSES

... You can ask the workingman in Ohio, you can ask a good cab driver in California, you can ask a clerk in Indiana, and you'll find that the masses of everyday people are very dissatisfied with the trends in this country .

Interview
U. S. News and World
Report
March 20, 1967

McCARTHYISM

... Many of his (the late Wisconsin Senator Joseph McCarthy) warnings about left-wingism and communism have proved valid. Maybe he was just a little ahead of his time.

Presidential Primary
Campaign
Appleton, Wisconsin
1964

MIDDLE EAST

... Whatever settlement that comes about (in the Middle East) ought to be what gives us some lasting peace in that area. We've had a war every ten years in the Middle East and it always threatens to bring confrontation between the major powers and I don't have any specifics about the settlement but whatever settlement is worked out it ought to be a lasting one if at all possible.

Press Conference
Greenville, South
Carolina
July, 1967

MILITARY POLICY

... As President (of the United States) I would lean heavily on the Joint Chiefs of Staff for military advice.

Newsweek
July 10, 1967

MOB RULE

... We are subjected to roving bands of irresponsible street rioters who are encouraged to break the laws by the irresponsible power gatherers in Washington, who themselves have violated the Constitution, broken the law, and now depend upon engendering irresponsibility in others for their support. We are faced with the astounding spectacle for the first time in a civilized nation, of high officials calling for the passage of a so-called Civil Rights Bill for fear of threat of mob violence—a mob movement which includes at least several communist-indoctrinated leaders.

Speech
Whitewater State College
Wisconsin
March 23, 1964

·· N ··

NAZISM

...I am an anti-Nazi. I fought Nazism in World War II, and I think it was one of the worst philosophies ever engendered in the world. I repudiate the support of anyone who says he wants to return to Nazism.

Interview
Meet The Press
(NBC-TV)
April 23, 1967

NEGRO

...The people of the United States do not hate the Negro. They have carried him on their shoulders and have endowed him with every blessing of civilization that he has been able to assimilate. They want him to rise just as high as his capacities and his industry will carry him, and the higher he rises, the lighter will be their load and the happier their hearts.

Speech
Harvard University
November 11, 1963

... Southern. When we speak of the Negro ✓ in the South, the image in our minds is that great residue of easy-going, basically happy, unambitious African, who constitutes 40% of our population, and who the white man of the South, in addition to educating his own children, has attempted to educate, to furnish public health services and civil protection.

Speech
Harvard University
November vv, vtfc

NEGROES

... I don't fear Negroes. I have lived with them all my life. Negroes have supported me in previous political campaigns and quite a few have told me they oppose the Civil Rights Bill.

Speech
Vincennes University
Indiana
April 21, 1964

... I never said a mean word about the Negro people, and I never will. You'd be amazed at how many friends Lurleen and I can count among the Negro voters. Why, in some of the big colored precincts of Birmingham, she polled a third of the votes and more. You look at the records. She lost Greene County by half a dozen votes—that's where that Black Panther crowd was operating—but look at Lowndes, Hale, Dallas, Marengo, Perry, Wilcox. They had federal examiners signing up every Negro in sight. There's a quarter of a million Negro voters in Alabama, and a whole lot of them voted for Lurleen.

Interview with James
Jackson   Kilpatrick
National Review
April 21, 1964

... **Alabama.** Alabama Negroes are not mistreated. There are over 105,000 now registered to vote and there are more Negro businessmen in Birmingham alone than there are in the entire state of New York.

Speech
Vincennes   University
Indiana
April 21, 1964

...We have hundreds of letters here pointing out what we have done for the Negro citizens of Alabama in the matter of our industrial-development program and supplied thousands of jobs. We've built the finest network of junior colleges and trade schools to serve them,

99

provided a free-textbook program through the twelfth grade for their children.

> *Interview*
> *U. S. News and World*
> *Report*
> *March* 20, 1967

...Employment. There is less non-white unemployment in Alabama and the southern states than there is in any FEPC state in the Union. There is more non-white employment in Alabama than there is in any FEPC state in the Union.

> *Speech*
> *Earlham College*
> *April* 20, 1964

...Juries. Negroes have served on juries (in the South) ever since I can remember. I was a judge for six years, and Negroes were on the jury, venire and drawn, and were on the panel for every court session that I held, and that was long before the passage of any so-called Civil Rights Act. Negroes served on juries, and they are entitled to serve on juries.

> *Interview*
> *Meet The Press*
> *(NBC-TV)*
> *April* 23, 1967

100

... **Segregation.** We invite the Negro citizen of Alabama to work with us from his separate racial station, as we will work with him, to develop, to grow in individual freedom. We want jobs and a good future for both our races. We want to help the physically and mentally sick of both races, the tubercular and the infirm. This is the basic heritage of my religion, of which I make full practice, for we are all the handiwork of God.

Inaugural Address
Montgomery, Alabama
January 14, 1963

... **Voting.** Negroes are entitled to vote. All citizens are entitled to vote, and any man who conforms to the requirements of a state law is entitled to vote, and they should be applied without discrimination.

Interview
Meet The Press
(NBC-TV)
April 23, 1967

··O··

OFFICIALS

...It's only natural that people in public office sometimes become unpopular because of the issues of the day.

Interview
U. S. News and
World Report
March 20, 1967

··P··

PACIFISTS

...(Pacifists) don't want to fight the Vietcong but they will fight the police.

New York Times
May 5, 1967

POLICE BRUTALITY

...I have always been against brutality, and those charges have been lodged with every police force in every large city in every state in the Union. And if we . . . were stampeded into doing away with all policemen that have been charged with police brutality, there would hardly be enough policemen in the United States to have traffic control. I am against police brutality; I have always been so—but only if it is true police brutality and not just some trumped-up charge.

Interview
Face The Nation
(CBS-TV)
March 14, 1965

PICKETS

. . . I have no objection to pickets. That's part of the American heritage.

Speech
Earlham College
Richmond, Indiana

POLITICAL PARTIES

. . . I believe that there is a ground swell of popular opinion against the course of both major parties of such proportions that they will get a real shock.

Interview
U. S. News and
World Report
March 20, 1967

... If both of the national parties continue on their present trend then it doesn't make much difference which one is elected.

Press Conference
Greenville, S. C.
July, 1967

... The average man on the street is concerned and disgusted with both national parties.

Press Conference
Greenville, S. C.
July 19, 1967

... The attitude of the leadership of both national parties is that there will not be a choice, and we in effect will have still a one-party system in 1968.

Interview
Meet The Press
(*NBC-TV*)
April 23, 1967

... I'm going to spoil the chances of both major parties, because they spoiled the chances of the people.

Newsweek
May 8, 1967

. . . The leadership of both national parties is the same. There's not any difference in the national Republicans and the national Democrats. In other words, it's Tweedledee and Tweedledum. We need a two-party system in the United States; we've got a one-party system now.

Interview
U. S. News and
  World Report
March 20, 1967

. . . **Conservatism.** When I entered the Presidential preferential primaries in the three states, I told the nation that my purpose was to help conservatize both national parties, and to get a message to the leadership of both parties, to return this country to the governmental principles upon which it was founded, and to cause the political leaders to think more of states' rights and local government; to bring a halt to this destruction of individual liberty and freedom.

Interview
Face The Nation
  (CBS-TV)
July 19, 1964

. . . My mission (in entering Presidential primaries in 1964) has been accomplished. My purpose was to help conservatize both national parties. Today we hear more talk of states' rights than we have heard in the past quarter century. I was the instrument through which the message was sent to the high councils of the parties.

Time Magazine
July 31, 1964

POLITICS

...**Average Man.** (The Wallace for President) movement is a movement of the people, and it doesn't make any difference whether top leading politicians endorse this movement or not. I think that if the politicians get in the way in 1968, a lot of them are going to get run over by this average man on the street, this man in the textile mill, this man in the steel mill, this barber, the beautician, the policeman on the beat. They are the ones—and the little businessmen—I think those are the mass of people that are going to support a change on the domestic scene in this country.

Interview
Meet The Press
(NBC-TV)
April 23, 1967

... **Parties.** Whether a candidate (for the United States Presidency) would be acceptable (to me) would also depend upon the platform of the party, and I don't think the (Republican) Party is going to give a platform to the American people that is much different from what the Democratic Party will give them. But if they want to stop a third-party movement, let them tell the American people that we are going to return our domestic institutions to you, we are going to get out of the business of the states, we are going to let the states and Alabama and California and any other state determine those policies, and then we will make that decision.

Interview
Meet The Press
(NBC-TV)
April 23, 1967

... **Presidential Candidates.** Now you take a big sack and you put LBJ in there, and you put Hubert Horatio Humphrey in there, and you put Bobby Kennedy, the blood-giver, in there, and you shake 'em all up. Then you put this Richard Milhous Nixon who with Eisenhower put bayonets in the backs of the people of Little Rock and in your backs, and you put in Earl Warren, who doesn't have enough legal brains in his head to try a chicken thief in my home county, and you shake 'em all up. And then you put in that Socialist Nelson Rockefeller from the most liberal state in the country, and that left-winger George Romney who was out in the streets with the demonstrators, and that Clifford Case of New Jersey, and that Wild Bill Scranton of Pennsylvania, and that radical Jacob Javits of New York, and you shake 'em all up. Then you turn that sack over, and the first one that falls out, you pick him up by the nape of the neck and drop him right back in again, because there's not a dime's worth of difference in any of 'em, national Democrats or national Republicans.

Quoted by
Jules Witcover
The Reporter
February 23, 1967

PRAYER

... We are concerned with the fact that today the (Supreme) Court has decided that no longer can you say a simple prayer in a public school because that violates, they say, the Constitution of our country. I don't know how we got along for 175 years with common sense, being able to say, "God we thank you

108

for the many blessings," but now many states have had to prohibit this saying as a result of that decision. The children bowing their heads in the public lunch room in the public schools, and saying, "God is great, God is good, God we thank you for our food." They say that's unconstitutional. I believe in the separation of church and state. But separation of state and God are two different things and there's nothing unconstitutional about bowing your head in a lunch room with little children and saying "God is great; God is good; God, we thank you for our food."

Speech
Rose Polytechnic Institute
Terre Haute, Indiana
Spring, 1967

PRESIDENCY

... There's no reason why someone from Alabama wouldn't make just as good a President as somebody from New York or maybe even Texas.

New York Times
Magazine
April 24, 1966

PRESIDENTIAL CAMPAIGN

... My campaign (for United States Presi-

dency) will be financed by millions of people
. . . Men in the street, little folks who are
going to send us contributions.

Interview
Meet The Press
(NBC-TV)
April 23, 1967

PRESIDENTIAL ELECTION

. . . To those who say you create a constitutional crisis if you throw (the Presidential
election) into the House of Representatives,
maybe a constitutional crisis in this regard
might help straighten the country out.

Press Conference
Greenville, S C.
July, 1967

. . . **Plurality.** I believe that if I am a candidate (for United States President in 1968)
that I can win because in 1964 I received 34%
of the primary vote in the state of Wisconsin without any campaign, without any organization, and if you got 34% of the total
vote in Wisconsin in 1968 and the other 66
are divided equally, 33 apiece among the
Republicans and Democrats you would win
the electoral vote of that state. When three
or more are running, it doesn't take a majority
to win, you win on a plurality. So in my

judgment, the philosophy that I espouse, the discontent about take-over of domestic institutions, the break-down of law and order, the matter of wasteful expenditures of money in some of the programs in our country involving foreign aid and others—there's so much opposition to this that if I am a candidate I could get a plurality not only in the state of South Carolina, but states above the Mason and Dixon line as well.

Press Conference
Greenville,
South Carolina
July, 1967

... It doesn't take a majority of the vote in any state when there are three or more candidates running for the Presidency to carry that state. A plurality wins. Thirty-four percent could conceivably win, and I received that many votes in the Democratic primary in Wisconsin three years ago.

Interview
Meet The Press
(NBC-TV)
April 23, 1967

PRESS

... The press in this country draws conclusions that have no foundation at all. And I think the American people are sick and tired of columnists and TV dudes who get on the national network and, instead of reporting the news as it is, which is what they are supposed to do, try to slant and distort and malign and brainwash this country. And I think that the American people haven't been brainwashed. And I think that the press and the national news media are going to get some of these liberal smiles wiped off their faces.

Interview
Face The Nation
(CBS-TV)
July 19, 1964

. . . The press doesn't occupy the place in American society it once did, and the reason is that many newspapers have failed to meet the demands of responsible reporting. People used to say they knew it was so because they read it in the newspaper, but you don't hear that said anymore.

Speech
Central Ohio Chapter
Sigma Delta Chi
Columbus, Ohio
February 12, 1964

. . . **News Management.** This nation's public information facilities . . . unfortunately

112

have in the majority, claimed freedom for the press, but have forgotten what freedom of the press really means—a dedication to supply not distortions of America, not a zeal to manage the people's thinking, but rather a duty to supply the facts to the people, in the faith that the American people have the decency and the consummate wisdom to reach decisions in the best interest of their country when given those unvarnished facts. Somewhere along the way news management to the people has become synonymous with political management of the people.

> *Speech*
> *Whitewater State College*
> *Wisconsin*
> *March 23, 1964*

PROGRESS

... It's from dissatisfaction that we get progress.

> *Press Conference*
> *Cincinnati, Ohio*
> *February 11, 1964*

... I am for progress. We have had the largest road-building program in Alabama's history; we have had the largest school-building program in Alabama's history.

Interview
U. S. News and
World Report
March 20, 1967

PROPAGANDA

... We are involved in a war for the minds of people—our people. We are living in a new kind of warfare—a warfare of propaganda that is waged unceasingly and ruthlessly. It is a warfare of which we know little and, sadly, in which we hold small skills. We must make the decisions now to stand up for America in our internal affairs. We must not be emotionalized into giving up the last bastion of freedom.

Speech
Whitewater State College
Wisconsin
March 23, 1964

PROPERTY RIGHTS

... Property rights are human rights, too, and the Civil Rights Bill threatens the destruction of property rights.

Meeting With Protestant
Ministers
Oshkosh, Wisconsin
April, 1964

114

... Every college I have been to with few exceptions I am asked this question: "Should-not you put human rights above property rights?" That sounds good. They put human rights above property rights in China and Russia. And in no country in the world where ownership of property is not guaranteed as sacred under the basic law is there any individual liberty and freedom. Human rights come first in Russia and China and the state owns all the property. In this country we have property rights and there are more individual liberties and freedoms in our country than exist in Russia and China. And nations in which you do have those rights are where you can own property. Don't you think one of the most basic of human rights is to own s o m e t h i n g some day and call it your own? Your home or business, isn't that a human right? Property rights are human rights. In my judgment when the property-ownership system is destroyed, you will have destroyed the liberty and freedom and human rights of all the people of our country regardless of who they happen to be.

Speech
Rose Polytechnic
Institute
Terre Haute, Indiana
Spring, 1967

... The only place where there are no human rights is the place where there are no property rights.

Speech
University of Cincinnati
Cincinnati, Ohio
February 11, 1964

PROTEST VOTE

... The large number of votes I received in the Wisconsin Presidential primary in 1964 was a protest vote against big government's trying to solve every problem every community faces. It was a protest against the Civil Rights Bill, which is an attack upon the free enterprise system of private ownership of property.

Interview
U. S. News and World
Report
April 20, 1964

··R··

RACE ISSUE

. . . Nobody in Alabama gets anywhere if he slants an election campaign to the racial issue.
                              Speech
                              John Hopkins University
                              Baltimore, Maryland
                              May 9, 1964

RACE RELATIONS

. . . **Hypocrisy.** The Negro people of America could expect if I were President, I would be genuinely concerned. Many of the people in other parts of the country have paid lip service to aiding people because of race but they are hypocritical. In Washington, D. C., for instance, we find that the school system is 94% Negro and six percent white. Because all of these hypocritical talking bureaucrats have gone to Virginia or Maryland or put their children in private schools. And the Negro citizens of this country would know that there's no such hypocrite in the President's office if I were there.

Press Conference
Greenville, South Carolina
July, 1967

RACES

... **Separation.** Each race, within its own framework has the freedom to teach, to instruct, to develop, to ask for and receive deserved help from others of separate racial station. This is the great freedom of our American founding fathers, but if we amalgamate into the one unit as advocated by the Communist philosophy, then the enrichment of our lives, the freedom for our development is gone forever. We become, therfore, a mongrel unit of one under a single all-powerful government. And we stand for everything and for nothing.

Inaugural Address
Montgomery, Alabama
January 14, 1963

RACIAL DISTURBANCES

... In the South, we believe in segregation and say so. In other sections of the country, including Milwaukee, where integration is supposed to be in force, Negroes are demonstra-

118

ting and threatening boycotts because they claim that segregation is still a way of life. I challenge you to visit Chicago, Baltimore, New York and some of the other large Northern cities and then come to Alabama and see for yourself if there isn't more racial peace than in any city in the North.

> *Meeting with Protestant*
> *Ministers*
> *Oshkosh, Wis.*
> *April,* 1964

.... Many out-of-state politicians are misleading our Negro citizens. They entice them with milk-and-honey talk into moving into no jobs and poor housing. These politicians must share the blame for racial troubles in their areas.

> *Speech*
> *University of Oregon*
> *January* 13, 1964

RACISM

... I've never made a racist speech in my life.

> *Interview*
> *U. S. News and World*
> *Report*
> *March* 20, 1967

... Life is too short to dislike people because of their race, color, creed or national origin and I would feel sorry for a person who dislikes a man for his color if he were to die at this moment because I think he wouldn't have a nice after-life.

Speech
Earlham College
Richmond, Indiana
April 20, 1964

... No one voted for me in the 1964 Presidential primary who is anti-Negro. I am not myself, and I ran no such campaign, nor have I ever run a campaign that was anti-Negro.

Interview
U. S. News and World
Report
June 1, 1964

... **and Segregation.** A racist is one who despises someone because of his color, and an Alabama segregationist is one who conscientiously believes that it is in the best interest of Negro and white to have a separate educational and social order.

Interview
U. S. News and World
Report
April 20, 1964

RED CHINA

...I would not admit Red China (to the United Nations.) I would be against admitting Red China until Red China shows that she is interested in peace. At the present time she is interested in world conquest.

Press Conference
Greenville, S. C.
July, 1967

RELIGION

...I am a Christian Theist.

Christian Century
April 21, 1965

...In a democracy the sovereign political power rests in the people, the United States Supreme Court to the contrary, notwithstanding. And while the Court may coerce with its awesome powers of contempt and trial without jury, it cannot brow-beat the American people into submission to the dictates of a Godless government ruled by agnostics and atheists. We will not permit God and religion to be suppressed, outlawed and banned from the institutions created by the people. Nor will we per-

mit the state or any branch of our government
to order God out of your neighborhood schools.

Testimony before the
House Judiciary
Committee
Washington, D. C.
April 21, 1964

... Spiritual vs. Material. Though we may
give lip service to the Almighty, in reality, government has become our God . . . It is a system that is the very opposite of Christ. It assumes the responsibilities that we ourselves
should assume. Its pseudo-liberal spokesmen
and some Harvard advocates have never exam-
ined the logic of its substitution of what it
calls "human rights" for individual rights, for
its propaganda plays upon words that have ap-
peal for the unthinking. Its logic is totally material and irresponsible as it runs the full
gamut of human desires, including the theory
that everyone has voting rights without the
spiritual responsibility of preserving freedom.
Our founding fathers recognized those rights,
but only within the framework of those spiritual responsibilities. But the strong, simple
faith and sane reasoning of our founding fathers has long since been forgotten as the so-
called "progressives" tell us that our Constitu-

tion was written for "horse and buggy" days. So were the Ten Commandments.

Inaugural Address
Montgomery, Alabama
January 14, 1963

RESPECT

... One of the great things necessary today in international affairs and foreign policy is to gain respect of peoples in all parts of the world and you gain respect by strength and honesty and straightforwardness. And we in this country have gotten to the point where we want to get a consensus of opinion about how somebody thinks about us 15,000 miles away. I think we ought to not worry about what people 15,000 miles away think of us, we ought to let them worry about what we think of them because most of our money goes to support most of them. Not that I don't care about peoples in other parts of the world because I do, but if they can't love us, let's make them respect us.

Press Conference
Greenville, S. C.
July, 1967

RIOTS

... If rioters knew they would get swift punishment, they would not throw that brick.

Press Conference
Greenville, S. C.
July 19, 1967

... If it takes riots to enhance my situation, I don't want it. I hope I get no more help from that source.

Quoted by Vera Glaser
North American
*   Newspaper Alliance*
August 27, 1967

124

·· S ··

SCHOOL APPROPRIATIONS

. . . **Alabama.** Exactly the same amount of money is appropriated for all children in Alabama, regardless of race, but it is based on the average daily attendance in each school. Unfortunately, there are a great many drop-outs in the Negro schools and, for that reason, they do not get as much as othe schools where attendance is higher.

Interview
Chicago Television
Program
February, 1964

SCHOOLS

. . . Bad-faith demogogues from other sections of the country spout off about our social order in the South for purely partisan political reasons when they can't control a bunch of hoodlums in their own school systems.

Opening Speech
1958 *Campaign for Governor of Alabama*
February 14, 1958

... The Federal Government has no business putting pressure on the local school system in New York or California, and if I were the President, that pressure would stop, and I'd pull every HEW official or bureaucrat or underling who was trying to force this on the people of New York or Alabama, I'd pull them out of the states and say, "You leave the business of running the schools to the respective states of our Union."

Interview
Meet The Press
(NBC-TV)
April 23, 1967

... Many people are concerned about neighborhood schools, because they know that the attempt is being made to destroy the neighborhood-school policy in order to satisfy the social whims of some social engineers.

Interview
U. S. News and World
Report
June 1, 1964

... If the people of a state cannot decide what is in the best interest of their own children without having to have the guidelines a thousand miles away, then you'd best, of course, abolish your cities and your states.

Speech
Rose Polytechnic Institute
Spring, 1967

...I am for Alabama determining the policy of her school system. And if she feels that in the best interests of both races a certain type system should exist, then that system should exist. The State of New York should determine the policies of her school system.

Interview
U. S. News and World
Report
March 20, 1967

...**Bible Reading.** Did you know that, as a result of the decision of the Federal Court about the Bible reading, a Board of Education has ruled that no longer can you sing the fourth stanza of *America* in the public schools of New York because it violates the decision of the Supreme Court of the United States regarding Bible reading and alluding to God?

Speech
Earlham College
Richmond, Indiana
April 20, 1964

. . . Federal Interference. I told the people of Wisconsin that we did not recommend segregation in their schools. We only recommended that they themselves set the policies for their own schools, without having "social engineers" from Washington trying to run them or set the policies under which they are run.

Interview
U. S. News and World
Report
April 20, 1964

. . .Local Control. If you want the neighborhood schools taken over by the Federal Government in Indiana and students transported across the city in Indianapolis and Terre Haute and Gary, then you're for the (Civil Rights) bill. But if you want that done by the local people here, then you ought to be against the bill. I make no recommendation to you in this state on that matter. I only recommend that you do it yourselves, and not let some social engineer 1,000 miles away in Washington do it for you.

Speech
Earlham College
Richmond, Indiana
April 20, 1964

. . . We want to see that all citizens of our country prosper and do well but they can prosper and do better if the matter of school problems are handled locally instead of some theoretician in an ivory tower in Washington looking down his nose and telling the people of Greenville, South Carolina, "we know best." The people of Greenville know best themselves.

Press Conference
Greenville, S. C.
July, 1967

. . . I believe in segregation of the public school system in Alabama. I believe that's the best school system for the people of Alabama. I think it is better for both races in Alabama. But I recommend no sort of school system for South Carolina or North Carolina, I recommend only that the people of Greenville, of Spartanburg and of Asheville decide the kind of school system they want and if they want this kind of school system they should have it. But today we have bureaucrats with beards, a lot of them, and that's literally true, from Washington that are today determining where a child can go to school in Greenville and who can teach that child and what books that child can use and this is something that the American people are sick and tired of and it is a great issue . . . I believe in states' rights, local government, so I don't recommend any sort of school system for Mississippi or California. Only that Mississippians and Californians decide it themselves.

Press Conference
Greenville, S. C.
July, 1967

. . . Segregation. I shall ask the legislature to give me the right to assign pupils to schools which are threatened with integration, and when the court order comes, I am going to place myself, your Governor, in the position so that the federal court order must be directed against the Governor and not some lesser official. As your Governor, I shall resist any illegal federal court order even to the point of standing at the schoolhouse door in person, if necessary.

Speech
1962 *Campaign for*
Governor Alabama

. . . I believe that in Alabama a segregated school system is in the best interest of both races. I believe that Californians should decide themselves what type of school system they would want to have.

Interview
Meet The Press
(*NBC-TV*)
April 23, 1967

SEGREGATION

... I'm not running on a platform of segrega-✓
tion because I have never recommended segregation in the school system for any state other
than my own. You have what you want to have
in Indiana. You have integration or segregation or whatever you want to call it, as long
as you decide yourselves through your policy-
makers what you want to have. Don't let somebody from Alabama tell you how to run your
schools here, nor from Washington; nor do we
want anybody from here or Washington telling
us how to run our schools in Alabama.

Speech
Earlham College
Richmond, Indiana
April 20, 1964

... I believe in segregation all right, but I
believe in segregation here in Alabama. What
New York wants to do, that's New York's business. Same for Ohio. Same for Louisiana. Let
folks decide for themselves. I don't care whether the owner of a restaurant serves Negroes
or doesn't serve them. It's his business. Just
don't make him look after customers in his
own place against his will.

Interview with
James Jackson Kilpatrick
National Review
April 18, 1967

131

... Of course I believe in segregation. Everybody does when you get right down to it.

New York Times
Magazine
April 24, 1966

... Racism is evil, but there is a difference between a racist and a segregationist. Racism is disliking God's handwork because a person is another color. If a man is convinced in his heart, and I am, that segregation is in the best interest of both races, there is nothing immoral or sinful about it. I am an Alabama segregationist because we have found, as have others in other parts of the nation and world, that race-mixing where there are large numbers of each race simply does not work in the interest of anyone.

Meeting with Protestant Ministers
Oshkosh, Wisconsin
April, 1964

... **Alabama.** I will continue to fight for segregation in Alabama because it is based on our firm conviction of right, and because it serves the best interest of all our people.

Speech
1962 Campaign for Governor of Alabama

. . . Segregation is the best plan for Alabama because that's what the people ot the state want.

Press Conference
Greenville, South Carolina
July, 1967

. . . As Governor, I am the highest constitutional officer of the State of Alabama. I embody the sovereignty of this State and I will be present to bar the entrance of any Negro who attempts to enroll at the University of Alabama.

Upon Court Ruling that
the University of
Alabama Admit
Negro Students
May 21, 1963

SELF-DETERMINATION

. . . I believe that in Alabama the people of that state should determine the policies of their domestic institutions.

Interview
Meet The Press
(NBC-TV)
April 23, 1967

"SEPARATE BUT EQUAL" DOCTRINE

. . . In 1840, the Supreme Judicial Court of

Massachusetts determined that Boston had the power to provide for the instruction of colored children in separate schools and to prohibit their attendance at other schools. Thereafter the Fourteenth Amendment was adopted and that rule of law was adjudicated applicable still on literally more than a score of occasions by the Supreme Court—the separate but equal doctrine. But came the vote-rich Negro lawyers to this court of politicians and ex-governors, with blocs of convention votes and bleeding hearts in 1953 with the demand that they overturn the separate but equal doctrine. The South, where lives the real African, had spent of its slender means literally billions of dollars providing teachers and facilities relying upon the separate but equal rule of law.

Speech
Harvard University
November 11, 1963

SIN

. . . Sin emanates from the heart.

Speech
Earlham College
Richmond, Indiana
April 20, 1964

134

SLAVERY

...I do not believe in slavery. I believe that all mankind was made in the image of God and I believe that He loves all of us and I believe that He loves one just as well as He does the other.

Speech
Earlham College
Richmond, Indiana
April 20, 1964

SOCIALISM

...The left-wingers want to guide this nation straight to socialism.

Speech
1964 *Presidential Primary*
Campaign
Cambridge, Maryland

SOCIAL RESPONSIBILITY

...It is the responsibility of mankind to care for the needy, the sick and the helpless.

Speech
1962 *Campaign for*
Governor of Alabama

SOCIAL SECURITY

...Social Security is a fact of American life,

and I'm all in favor of taking care of the old folks.

Interview with
James Jackson Kilpatrick
National Review
April 18, 1967

SOCIAL WELFARE

. . . Helping the elderly citizens of our state—75 and 80, 90 years old—who are indigent is not a giveaway program. It's a humane program that's in the interest of all of us. And we've helped the blind and the sick and the disabled and tubercular in this state. We give textbooks to the children of Alabama. Those programs are good. They are "conservative" programs.

Interview
U. S. News and World Report
March 20, 1967

SOUTH

. . . Persons outside the South are not told the entire truth, just part of it . . . If we were as bad in the South as many of you have played up, I wouldn't want to go to school with the whites in the South myself.

Press Conference
Los Angeles, California
January 9, 1964

...I'm a professional Southerner.

New York Times
Magazine
April 23, 1966

... It is very appropriate . . . that from this
Cradle of the Confederacy, this very heart of
the great Anglo-Saxon Southland, that today
we sound the drum for freedom as have our
generations of forebearers before us time and
again down through history. Let us rise to the
call of the freedom-loving blood that is in us
and send our answer to the tyranny that clanks
its chains upon the South. In the name of the
greatest people that have ever trod this earth,
I draw the line in the dust and toss the gaunt-
let before the feet of tyranny . . . and I say . . .
segregation now . . . segregation tomorrow . . .
segregation forever.

Inaugural Address
Montgomery, Alabama
January 14, 1963

... **Economic Struggle.** Those who charge
Alabama and the South with discrimination,

are the same hypocrites who for so long discriminated against the South in an economic
way. Those people who want to destroy our
educational and social order are the same
people who want to destroy the free enterprise system in America.

Speech
Alabama State Chamber
of Commerce
Birmingham, Ala.
November 15, 1962

. . . **Political Importance.** We intend to take
the offensive and carry our fight for freedom
across the nation, wielding the balance of
power we know we possess in the Southland. . .
We, not the insipid block voters of some sections . . . will determine in the next election
who shall sit in the White House of these United States . . . from this hour . . . from this
minute . . . we give the word of a race of
honor that we will tolerate their boot in our
face no longer . . . and let those certain judges
put that in their opium pipes of power and
smoke it for what it is worth.

Inaugural Address
Montgomery, Alabama
January 14, 1963

. . . **Racial Policies.** Mississippi in the last √
five years has obtained more new industries

138

than any other state in the South except Flori-
da. Mississippi has conducted its racial affairs
on a sound and tranquil basis with peace and
dignity for both the white and Negro races.
Georgia, on the other hand, recently changed
its racial policy to admit racial integration, and
what did they get? They got sit-ins, shoot-ins,
fall-ins and all sorts of other racial disturbances
and crimes. I say that I choose to follow Mississippi's example and not the example set by
Georgia.

> *Speech*
> 1962 *Campaign*
>   *Run-off Election for*
>   *Governor of Alabama*

...School System. I am going to stand up
against those who would try to take over our
school system . . . I'm going to wake the
country up. I believe that's the destiny of
the people of this state—and that's to save
this nation.

> *Speech*
> 1962 *Campaign for*
>   *Governor of Alabama*

SOUTH AMERICA

...We should help the people of South
America with technology and progress of that
sort, and education. You can pour money into

a place where you have low education and a high illiteracy rate . . . every year and every year and if that's all you do, fortunes will be spent and you'll still be at a standstill. I do think that we should help in every way we could, those of our South American neighbors, in a realistic way. Don't just pour money there to be pouring it, because one hundred years from now you'll still be pouring it, and they'll be in the same position they are. I think we ought to help them in the matter of technology and the matter of education.

Speech
Earlham College
Richmond, Indiana
April 20, 1964

SOUTHERNERS

. . . I have had just as much experience in American political life as Mr. Romney, Mr. Nixon, or Mr. Johnson have had, and when I go to the National Governors Conferences, I don't take a backseat to the Governor of Michigan or New York or California—no disrespect to them. I represent just as good and fine a people as they do. And governors from my region are just as intelligent and just as knowledgable as the governors of these other

states. So why shouldn't the Governor of
Alabama want to run for President, if he
wants to run? After all, that is a right that
we have, although I know that many people
. . . think that it is ludicrous for a Southerner
to want to run for President. Yet some of
the best Presidents we have ever had have
come from our great region of the country.

> *Interview*
> *Meet The Press*
> *(NBC-TV)*
> *April 23, 1967*

STATE GOVERNMENT

. . . **Honesty.** There's only one type of state
government that can meet the challenge of
the times—state government that is honest
and incorruptible.

> *Speech*
> *Meeting of the*
> *   Montgomery County*
> *   Wallace for Governor*
> *   Volunteers*
> *January 22, 1962*

. . . I shall fulfill my duty toward honesty
and economy in our state government so that
no man shall have a part of his livelihood

cheated and no child shall have a bit of his
future stolen away.

Inaugural Address
Montgomery, Alabama
January 14, 1963

STATES' RIGHTS

... When it gets down to the lick log, as
we rednecks in Alabama say, the people of
(the State of) Washington will vote against
something which affects them personally, just
as we do in Alabama. And if the people of
Washington want to remove racial and religious imbalance, as required by the pending
Civil Rights Bill, that's fine. But let the people
of Washington or of Seattle do it—not some
socio-political theorist in Washington (D. C.)
4,000 miles away.

Speech
University of Washington
January 14, 1964

... I do not recommend segregation in any
phase of our society in any state in this Union.
I only recommend that the states of the Union
continue to determine the policies of their
domestic institutions themselves and that the
bureaucrats and the theoreticians in Washington let people in Ohio and New York and

142

California decide themselves for instance what type of school system they are going to have. I recommend states' rights and local government. Territorial democracy is what I recommend.

Interview
Meet The Press
(NBC-TV)
April 23, 1967

... It's the right of the state to protect the safety, health and morals of its people.

Speech
Baton Rouge, Louisiana
September 2, 1967

... The gathering of absolute power by men, into a central body of government, was greatly feared by the founding fathers of this country. With rights and powers divided among separate state governments, close to and answerable to the citizens of each state, no single group could hope to gain control over the people. But with the rights and powers of the states destroyed, with power centralized into one seat of control, tyranny, benevolent or otherwise, is assured over the people.

Speech
Whitewater State College
March 23, 1964

STUBBORNNESS

. . . Anybody who pushes any movement to a point of engendering ill will is not helping solve any problem.

Interview
U. S. News And
World Report
April 20, 1964

SUPREME COURT

. . . The United States Supreme Court legislates when it ought to be adjudicating. We are run by an oligarchy of men that are appointed for life and not elected to office.

Speech
Earlham College
Richmond, Indiana
April 20, 1964

. . . **Justices.** Today you will look in vain at the nine (Supreme Court justices) . . . on that bench for a single man whose outstanding legal ability will explain his presence on the court—rather they are there, and you can identify them, one by one, with one possible exception, because they are strong with labor or represent racial or religious blocs or because they are New Deal, New Frontier or, as a state political figure, controlled some votes at a Presidential nominating convention. Some of this, of course, has happened before, but never in our history has it happened that the Court lacks a single man distinguished as a lawyer before his calling to the bench— that each man carried to the Court with him a cause to serve other than the cause of justice, justice under law.

Speech
Harvard University
November 11, 1963

· · T · ·

TAXES

... People are getting sick and tired of bureaucrats, in effect, telling them when they can go to bed at night, when they can get up in the morning. These government people have become involved in business operations, in labor unions, in hospitals and schools and every other local democratic institution. I'm not against the government's doing some of the things it does, such as the matter of highway construction. I'm not against the government's providing aid to education, because that money is not federal money; it's taxpayers' money. It comes from the pockets of the people all the way from California to New York.

Interview
U. S. News and
World Report
March 20, 1967

THIRD-PARTY MOVEMENT

... In a third-party movement it doesn't take

146

a majority to win—it takes a plurality.

Interview
U. S. News and
World Report
March 20, 1967

... Most every major party this country has had used to be a third party. Each of our two major parties today developed originally from a third party. So there's a good chance, with the sentiment in the country today, that a third-party movement could in turn become the major party.

Interview
U. S. News and
World Report
March 20, 1967

... The whole purpose of this (third-party) movement is to make one of the national parties decide that it's going to change to give the people a choice. And if they do that, then we feel we have accomplished our purpose.

Interview
October, 1967

TREASON

... The first thing we ought to do now is to impress Hanoi, Moscow and Peking that the American people are solidly behind this war. I respect the right of dissent all right, but anybody who undertakes to give aid to the Vietcong is engaged in treason. That's the way I see it. I'd order the Justice Department to proceed against them, indict them, try them. And if any judges tried to say it isn't *legally* treason, because we aren't formally at war, I'd get some new judges. They wouldn't be judges like Earl Warren, either, who sits there and applauds the President while he talks about bills the Court will have to pass on.

Interview with
James Jackson Kilpatrick
National Review
April 18, 1967

TRIAL BY JURY

. . . One of the most devastating effects of the (Civil Rights) bill is that it destroys the right of trial by jury. If your grandmother runs a boarding house and she is found guilty of discrimination under this bill, she can be sent to the penitentiary without a trial. How can it be a civil rights bill when it destroys

the most basic of all civil rights, that of a
trial by a jury of your peers?

Speech
Indiana University
Bloomington, Indiana
April 23, 1964

TRUTH

... Truth will ultimately prevail ... Today
every news medium of national importance,
every powerful politician, and particularly the
political elements of the courts, are against
us. That is a mighty combination, but they
cannot in the end prevail over simple, plain
truth. It may be five years, it may be ten
years, but like the prohibition amendment,
this error will pass from the scene and truth
and sanity will ultimately prevail.

Speech
Harvard University
November 11, 1963

... Patriotic Americans have a great duty
before them. It is a duty that will require
patience, persistence and courage. We must
have patience to continually point to the truth.
We must exercise that patience even in the
most violent storm of recriminations against
us by those who seek through centralized
authority to vanquish freedom in the name

of freedom; to destroy human rights and dignity in the name of civil rights; to inspire hatred and chaos in the name of love and peace.

Speech
Whitewater State College
Wisconsin
March 23, 1964

TYRANNY

... The heel of tyranny does not fit the neck of an upright man.

Inaugural Address
Montgomery, Alabama
January 14, 1963

··U··

UNITED NATIONS

...I doubt if the United Nations will ever do anything.

Press Conference
Greenville,
South Carolina
July 19, 1967

...The United Nations is interfering too much in things that it ought not to be getting into.

Interview with
James Jackson Kilpatrick
National Review
April 18, 1967

...I'm not for surrendering one iota of sovereignty ... to any international body.

Press Conference
Greenville, S. C.
July, 1967

...I would lead a movement for some re- ✓ forms in the United Nations to stop it from being a propaganda factor for the Communists in our country and some reforms that would allow a few small nations that you've never heard of to control some policy in our own country.

Press Conference
Greenville, S. C.
July, 1967

... The United Nations is not much of an institution as far as I'm concerned, but let's hope that they can do one thing in their existence that amounts to something and that's to bring about some settlement in the Middle East.

Press Conference
Greenville, S. C.
July, 1967

$\cdot\cdot\mathrm{V}\cdot\cdot$

VIETNAM

. . . I think we've got to pour it on (in Vietnam). We've got to win this war. If that means stepping up the bombing, step it up. If it means blocking off Haiphong, block her off. But there's no sense talking peace with that crowd until you've got them whipped. And I wouldn't put any of those Vietcong in a new government, either. First thing you know, they'd take it over. Then where would you be?

Interview with
James Jackson Kilpatrick
National Review
April 18, 1967

. . . Any Alabama student who takes the extreme line—like sending blood and money to the Vietcong, or burning his draft card, or urging our troops not to fight—we'll expel them. And that goes for any professors who want us to lose the war in Vietnam. Academic freedom! They talk about academic freedom, and tenure, and accreditation. They got the college presidents scared to death.

Interview with
James Jackson Kilpatrick
National Review
April 18, 1967

... I believe that the Vietnam war can be settled in a military fashion by the military and I would hope that we would escalate the bombings of the supply routes and of the harbor facilities of North Vietnam to stop the flow of supplies from China and Russia into North Vietnam. I think there can be a military conclusion in this matter.

Press Conference
Greenville, S. C.
July, 1967

... One of the first things I would do as President which I think would help in the Vietnam war is to show Hanoi and Peking and Moscow the determination and resolve of the people of this country in support of their servicemen. Now there are many good people who dissent about us being in Vietnam but we are in Vietnam and since we are there we should support wholeheartedly the American servicemen. And what I think we should do and what the Justice Department ought to to is to indict and put in the penitentiary folks in this country who are raising money and blood and clothes for the Vietcong Communists. And some of these professors in some of these colleges in our country who are advocating a victory of the Vietcong Communists over the American servicemen should be dragged figuratively by their beards before a federal grand jury and put in the penitentiary for what they are: traitors! I would stop overt acts of treason in this nation. I'm not talking about dissent. I believe in the right of dissent.

Press Conference
Greenville, S. C.
July, 1967

... (The Vietnam war is) the most important matter facing the American people and the whole free world.

Quoted by
Jules Witcover
The Reporter
February 23, 1967

... There can be a military solution (in Vietnam). We can de-escalate the war by escalating the bombing of North Vietnam.

Press Conference
Greenville, S. C.
July 19, 1967

. . . Treason. There are many fine people in our country who conscientiously believe that we should not be in Vietnam. They love this country and feel that our being there is a mistake but they are not against our being there because they love some other system. They are against it because they think it's not in our interest. But we are in Vietnam and today 400,000-odd young men and women are there committed between life and death against Communist aggression. And just because the theoreticians say there formally is no war we still have the right of freedom of speech which we do, and the right to dissent . . . (But) anyone who raises money and clothes and blood for the Vietcong, and college professors, as some have recently done, who stand and tell student bodies that they long for a victory of the Vietcong Communists over the American imperialist troops in the name of academic freedom, I say to you that is not academic freedom, that's treason.

Speech
Rose Polytechnic Institute
Terre Haute, Indiana
Spring, 1967

VIOLENCE

... I don't believe in violence as the solution of domestic problems.

Press Conference
Greenville, S. C.
July 19, 1967

VOTING

... We have thirteen statutes on the statute books of our nation that could have corrected the (voting requirements) inequities in a few counties in one state and a few counties in another state without taking away the right of the people of the states under the Constitution to determine voting rights and voting qualifications.

Interview
Meet The Press
(NBC-TV)
April 23, 1967

VOTING ACT

... I would ask that the Voting Act be repealed. I think one of the most tragic pieces of legislation in the country is a piece of legislation aimed at five states. There are only five states in the Union affected by the Voting Rights Act. An illiterate can vote in Alabama, South Carolina, Louisiana, Georgia and Mississippi, but if that same illiterate moves to the State of New York, he cannot vote. And that is unfair. Yes, I would ask that that be repealed.

Interview
Meet The Press
(NBC-TV)
April 23, 1967

WAR

... Strength, respect, and power are deterrents to war.

Newsweek
July 10, 1967

... I don't believe in war as an instrument of policy.

Press Conference
Greenville, S. C.
July, 1967

WEALTH

... Governments do not produce wealth. People produce wealth.

Inaugural Address
Montgomery, Alabama
January 14, 1963